Contents

PART THREE
THE STUDY OF SCOTLAND'S LANGUAGES
*Papers on the current study of and investigations into Gaelic,
Scots and Scottish Standard English.*

Foreword

On 15 November 1975 there was a one-day conference in the University of Glasgow on 'English As We Speak It In Scotland'. This meeting was so successful that it was followed by another in the same place on 13 November 1976 on 'Scotland's Languages: the Contemporary Situation'. The present volume contains revised and (in several cases) expanded versions of the papers given on these two occasions. Both conferences attracted a remarkable number of participants, not a few of whom were from England and overseas, and the meetings did not pass unnoticed by the Scottish press and radio. Their concerns were closely linked with those of several other, earlier, conferences and discussions devoted to related topics; a list of these is given at the end of Chapter 8.

Over the last decade there has been a marked increase in interest in various aspects of the contemporary language situation in Scotland and in its complex historical background. Above all there has been a growing awareness that the underlying problems have many interesting parallels, not only in Europe but in various other parts of the world as well. It was no accident that participants came from countries far from Scotland and that they raised basic questions that might have escaped attention in any more exclusively Scottish conclaves.

The holding of these and similar earlier conferences and the great interest they have aroused indicates more than a mere academic concern and an awareness that many of the matters discussed are of the greatest relevance to contemporary Scotland. It is hardly necessary to add that, underlying the conferences themselves, there are organisations and individuals, both on the Scots and the Gaelic side, working to ensure that the efforts of many persons over recent generations have not been in vain. It is particularly encouraging to see that a widespread understanding of the broader cultural issues now links the problems of Scots and Gaelic, and is more than ever emphasising the richness of a cultural heritage which in an inextricable way involves both and also links each in various linguistic and cultural ways with innumerable aspects of the European tradition as a whole.

My own first glimmerings of this go back close on half a century to the time when I first steeped myself in the writings of W P Ker. It is fitting in the present context to pay tribute to that great Glaswegian and to remind readers of this volume that the mere first paragraph of one single lecture of his (on *Don Quixote*) delivered seventy years ago to the Royal Philosophical Society of his native city is sufficient to give one a sense of what I have just been emphasising and what we must never lose sight of.

No-one with any experience of what has been going on in these directions in recent years can fail to have sensed the steadily growing interest in a massive complex of living cultural issues and their historical antecedents. This is something which it would be difficult to parallel in Scotland without going back to that remarkable period early in the nineteenth century when novelists and poets and editors of texts and antiquaries and historians and lexicographers all felt themselves to be part of one vital movement which transcended the particular interests of any of them. It is entirely fitting, and it is scarcely accidental, that in our own age, when in all sorts of ways the country is seeking to establish, and be more conscious of, its own deeper identity, a concern for living cultural roots should be making itself felt. It is also natural that linguistic questions should be seen as very central to the whole problem of identity and to the fuller and deeper understanding of so much that lies in our past but is yet still part of what we are.

As one who has for a long time now been occupied with some of the more academic aspects of such problems, I should not wish anyone to forget the huge efforts made over many decades which paved the way for some of the developments now taking place. It was said of Shakespeare by one of his grudging contemporaries that 'he but hatched the eggs that his elder friends laid'. Some of the 'elder friends' of the present oviparous movement are, alas, no longer with us. This is not the place to single out names, whether of Celticists or of Scots scholars or even of those whose interests straddled both disciplines. What is more important is the collective contribution of all these persons without whose often self-effacing and sometimes ill-recognised efforts we would not, today, have either the insights or the foundations of scholarly understanding on which, ourselves, to build. But if I speak of scholarly understanding we should also remember how much more than merely academic so large a part of what they strove for was, both in their own vision of it and in the actual outcome.

It is therefore good that some of these present papers link linguistic problems with various broader matters. It is still better that the trend which many were activating already in the first half of the century, a trend in which the great relevance of linguistic matters to contemporary Scottish life and society as a whole would gradually come, between then and now, to be more and more realised, is so clearly in evidence now. In the changes of attitude that have thus come about I should want (as Sir Walter Scott would have) to associate scholars and creative writers; nor should we forget that in the last resort the aspirations and attitudes of both groups (including often a healthy lack of unanimity) are in the main the product of deeper and but dimly understood forces at work among and around them.

Given this general advance in awareness and concern I see no special point in anyone attempting too zealously to control and steer the precise direction which it takes. What I should want to encourage and help to stimulate would be the gradual permeation of a fuller understanding of the matters we are here concerned with among more and more people. Some of my friends, I suspect, tend to confuse the promulgation of plans and policies with the fostering of a vaguer but deeper kind of sense of the whole tangled complex of our heritage and our present ways of life, in both of which language so centrally sits. Those best remembered a hundred years from now, be they poets or phoneticians, folk-singers or etymologists, will be those who, wittingly or unwittingly, have played a significant part in that fostering.

We should firmly realise in any case that things will by no means turn out exactly as this or that planner might have hoped. But if there is no neglect of a nurturing of informed awareness it may well be that the outcome will on balance be the better for that. So far as I believe in planning in relation to such matters as I am considering here, it is mainly in rather wearisome administrative and financial directions; the keywords here are 'convincing' and 'persuading' rather than anything I should describe as 'planning' in the full sense of this sadly abused word.

I naturally share the now widespread feeling that there ought to be a much profounder realisation at various governmental levels of the basic problems and needs, so that financial and other provision can—as a measure of plain common sense and of the highest survival-value—be made for our languages and their history and background and for the treasures, old and new, oral and written, which are preserved in them, to be adequately studied and taught and *treasured* at all levels from primary schools to the graduate departments of our universities.

We have no great reason, as a nation, to be smug about our achievement so far in these directions. Nor should we make the mistake of assuming that, in the hurly-burly of any considerable political change, official attitudes to such things are bound or even likely to take automatically a turn for the better. So we must be prepared to face obligations, and sometimes daunting and unpalatable tasks, in the direction of making sure that these attitudes do change. At least some of the groundwork for bringing about just this has, I think, been achieved by the recent series of deliberations on a number of central and fundamental problems; they should at least help to promote a gradual widening of public awareness of the importance of these problems. It is specially reassuring that this awareness can now more and more clearly be seen to extend far beyond the confines of Scotland; we are not ourselves the sole legatees of the Scottish linguistic inheritance.

This present volume provides an authoritative, and so far the only readily accessible, account of two central aspects of the overall linguistic situation. We may confidently look forward to other published work by writers who will approach these and similar topics from a variety of different points of view. Meanwhile I believe that what is set forth in the following pages will be of much interest and value to all those concerned with Scotland's rich and complex linguistic heritage and its relevance to the well-being and integrity of Scottish society and culture in the years ahead of us.

Angus McIntosh

Forbes Professor of English Language
University of Edinburgh

PART ONE

SCOTLAND'S LANGUAGES

*Papers on the history and present position
of Scotland's languages.*

1
The Historical Background

David Murison

What the first language of what is now Scotland was, we do not know, nor is there time to go into the much disputed intricacies of the Pictish question. For brevity's sake let us say that the earliest language of Scotland that we can understand is an early form of what is now Welsh, which we may call *British* in the original sense of the term. It was a branch of the Celtic languages, closely related to the language of Gaul and distinguished from the other main branch of Celtic, the Irish or Gaelic, by having the sound *p* where the other has *q* (written *c*), from an original *kw*. The remains of this tongue survive in place-names like *Leith, Innerleithen, Linlithgow, Glasgow, Traquair, Tranent, Ochiltree, Penicuik, Pencaitland, Peebles, Aberdeen, Aberdour, Abernethy* etc, and also in a peculiarly Scottish feature, the prefix *Pit-* (in *Pitscottie, Pitfour, Pittencrieff, Pitcox, Pittenweem, Pitsligo*), which may be the same word as English *piece* (from Gaulish through Latin and French) and possibly also *peat*.

The disappearance of this language is due to its being ousted by Gaelic or *q*-Celtic, which came from Ireland with the Scots in the late fifth century AD and spread from Dalriada in Argyll all over Pictland, that is Scotland north of the Forth, before AD 850. By AD 950 the speakers of this language had won the overlordship of the British kingdom of Strathclyde, and they ultimately extended the Gaelic language over the rest of Scotland except the south-east, as we can see from new place-names, for example *Kin-* in place of *Pen-* (*Kincardine, Kinross, Kinloch*) and *Inver-* for *Aber-* (*Inverness, Inveresk, Inverkeithing, Inverurie*) and, incidentally, from the *Book of Deer* (*c* 1150), the first written record of this language in Scotland.

It is, however, the remaining south-east part of Scotland between Forth and Tweed which concerns us most as the original home of the Scots tongue. Its history as an originally British-speaking region consists of unsuccessful attempts to contain invaders from the south who had established themselves in the Thames area about AD 450 and worked their way up the eastern side of England throughout the next century. These invaders were the Angles, one of two tribes from the lands of north-west Germany, the Angles from Slesvig and the other tribe, the Saxons, from further south. The Welsh and Irish Celts lumped them all together under the name Saxons, *Saeson, Sasunnaich*; it was the Angles, however, who gave their name to the country of England. They fanned northwards from the Thames through East Anglia, Yorkshire and Northumberland, where they founded the kingdom of Bernicia, based on Bamburgh, in AD 547. The northern limits of this kingdom reached the Forth in the course of the next century. The British fortress of Din Eidyn was captured by the Bernicians in AD 638 and their territory became established as far as Abercorn, just west of South Queensferry. There was also some penetration westward into Galloway, partly through the Anglic Church of Cuthbert which had succeeded the Celtic Church of Aidan at Lindisfarne; a bishopric was established near Wigtown with the Anglo-Saxon name of Whithorn (*hwīt ærn*, 'white house', Latinised as *Candida Casa*).

All this has been recorded in the histories of Bede and the Chronicles of Anglo-Saxons and Picts and Scots, but there is also the evidence of place-names of Anglo-Saxon origin in the south-east (especially East Lothian and Berwick), such as *Coldingham, Tyningham, Whittingehame, Haddington, Mordington, Ednam* (< *Edenham*), *Edrom* (< *Adderham*). Finally there is the tangible memorial of the Ruthwell Cross with its inscription of a few lines from *The Dream of the Rood*, an early Northumbrian poem. Dating from the early part of the eighth century, this is the first literary work in the language that still exists as Scots.

For the following three centuries we have little evidence of this northern Anglo-Saxon language. Historical records are few. We do know that in AD 973 Edgar, king of England, hard-pressed by Norsemen, ceded Lothian to the Scottish king, Kenneth II. With that treaty the boundaries of Scotland were extended more or less to what they are today, and we can assume that the Gaelic place-names found in the Lothian region are to be dated to this period. But obviously, in such a relatively populous area, Anglo-Saxon must have prevailed among the majority of the inhabitants. The Scottish court itself was becoming familiar with the language; King Malcolm

III (Canmore), for instance, had been at the English court of Edward the Confessor for fourteen years. Meanwhile, in England, the Danes had commenced their attacks on the north-east coast. They ultimately established a Norse kingdom, the Danelaw, at York in AD 867, which lasted with fluctuating fortunes for two centuries. Bernicia seems to have remained as a buffer state between Scotland and the Danes and there are few Norse place-names in Lothian. In the Solway area, however, there was considerable influence from Cumberland where Norwegians, coming immediately from Ireland, had invaded and settled. Typical Scandinavian place-name elements occur there, such as *-dale* (*Annandale, Nithsdale, Liddisdale*), *-by* (*Lockerbie, Canonbie, Middlebie*), *-thwaite*, *-gill*, *-beck*, all familiar in the Lake District; an interesting name is *Tinwald* near Dumfries, with which we may compare *Tynwald* in Man, *Dingwall* in Rossshire, *Tingwall* in Shetland and of course *Thingvellir* in Iceland. Above all, the Norsemen profoundly affected the speech of northern England by introducing a Scandinavian or Old Norse element into the sound system and vocabulary, which still strongly survives in modern Scots.

Norse is characterised by the absence of palatalisation of gutturals in connection with front vowels: where English has *ch* and *y*, and in some positions *-dge*, Norse retains *k* and *g*. Thus words like *ken, kettle, like, get, give, egg* are Norse loan-words in place of English *chen, chetel, liche, yet, yive, ey* (as in *Cockney*), which are now obsolete or specialised in some way. This phonological correspondence explains many of the distinctions between the Northern and Scots forms and the Southern and Standard English: *kirk, church*; *kirn, churn*; *muckle, much*; *breeks, breeches*; *dike, ditch*; *sic, such*; *ilk, each*; *brig, bridge*; *rig, ridge*; *sing, singe*; similarly with *sk* and *sh* as in *skirl, shrill*; *skriech, shriek*; *mask, mash*.

There are also differences arising from variations in vowel development, as in *lowp, leap*; *cowp* (to bargain), *cheap*; *nowt, neat*; *ain, own*; *strae, straw*; *hing, hang*; *trig, true*; and somewhat similarly *blae, blue*; *brae, brow*. In vocabulary, Scots has many Norse words such as *big* (build), *carline, eident, ferlie, frae, gar, flit, gowk, graith, host* (cough), *low* (flame), *lug, luif, kilt, maun, nieve, rowan, skug, stowp, tyke*. It is worth noticing the large proportion of these words still surviving in everyday use.

The great event which radically altered the speech of

England and, later, of Scotland was of course the Norman Conquest in 1066. The English royal family took refuge in Scotland and the Princess Margaret later married the widower king, Malcolm III. Over the next hundred years, the anglicisation of Scotland proceeded under the rule of Margaret and Malcolm and their three sons, Edgar, Alexander and David, who succeeded them. David I, in particular, used the feudal system, Church and trade through the new burghs as means to this end.

While the chief grantees of land from the Scottish Crown were undoubtedly French-speaking Normans—with names like Comyn, Bruce, Baliol, Morville, Sinclair, Fitzalan (the later Stewarts), Somerville and Grant—all of them had come via England, especially from North and East Midland England, the old Danelaw. What is more important, they brought with them their retainers and hangers-on—bailiffs, land-stewards and the like—who were English speakers, and settled them on the lands they had acquired. Similarly in the Church, while some of the chief ecclesiastics were Normans, many others were Englishmen, like Turgot, Queen Margaret's confessor, later Bishop of St Andrews. More Englishmen came with the many religious orders invited to Scotland by David, and we must infer that the parochial clergy trained by such men would have been English-speaking too.

The practical results of all this mixing of populations can be seen in the attestations to charters, where the several signatories may have Welsh, Gaelic, Norse, Anglo-Saxon and French names. Gaelic families tended to choose English or French names for their children; Celtic officials are followed by ones with non-Celtic names. The population must have become even more polyglot in the twelfth and thirteenth centuries, and we must suppose that the *lingua franca* of them all was the one that ultimately prevailed, the new, highly-Frenchified English.

But probably the most significant factor in anglicisation was the rise of the burghs, founded by David and his successors. There is abundant evidence from charters, burgess rolls and the like, that at the beginning many people with English names settled in the burghs, even in Inverness and in St Andrews, which was a last stronghold of the Celtic Church in the twelfth century. Significantly, the vocabulary of the burgh is basically Anglic or Anglo-Scandinavian: *burgh* itself, *toft, croft, rig, rood, alderman, gild, soc and sac, toll, gate* (street), *raw, wynd*; with some French additions like *provost, bailie, port, vennel, ferme.*

That English was taking over in the countryside too, in the old Celtic territories, is evident from the *new* place-names which began to appear *north* of the Forth in the early thirteenth century. The Celts had already given names to the chief geographical features—hills, rivers, lakes, rocks, valleys, marshes and so on, from which we derive our common nouns *ben, loch, glen, strath, craig, bog*—and these place-names were taken over by English speakers. But from Angus to Banffshire we can trace Anglic names like *Redefurd, Staneycroft, Stobstane,* and hybrid names like *Corncairn, Gledcairn, Crawcairn* which show that the word *cairn* had already been adopted into the English vocabulary of the region, all before 1220. These names could only have been given by the English-speaking officials or tenants of the local magnates.

The magnates themselves no doubt continued to speak French among themselves as the language of law, war and chivalry, and of culture, though as time went on they must have become bilingual as they did in England. One difference between Scotland's and England's practice of the period is noticeable, namely the Scottish use of Latin in state documents, whereas in England French was used. There is no evidence that French was used in the law courts in Scotland, but it was the regular practice in England, with interpreters in constant service. However, French was used for letters to the king and realm of England and it was significantly in common use throughout the English occupation of Edward I and the War of Independence, but was displaced again by Latin when that period was over.

After the mid-fourteenth century, the first signs of the vernacular reappear in written use: in glosses in a Latin charter, in deeds between the landed gentry, not to mention in some popular songs of which some fragments survive from the war. By the end of the century Sir James Douglas and the Earl of March were both writing to Henry IV of England in English, 'for', said the Earl, 'that is mare clere to myne understandynge than latyne or fraunche'. But of course French had left its indelible mark on the Anglo-Saxon it had temporarily displaced, by drastically simplifying its accidence, altering its syntax, modifying its spelling, and vastly enlarging and enriching its vocabulary, all of which in due course spilled over into Scotland.

The two main sources of French influence are Norman French, which lived on in England till the fourteenth century, and Central French, which came later, partly from the court of Henry II, Count of Anjou and afterwards King of England, and partly from the culturally prestigious French court at Paris. This is the underlying distinction between the French of Stratford atte Bow, spoken by Chaucer's Prioress, and the French of Paris. It explains the doublets in English of *cattle* and *chattel*, *catch* and *chase*, *ward* and *guard*; and to it can be traced some of the other differences between English and Scots forms, as *fail, failyie*; *spoil, spulyie*; *oil, ulyie*; *coin, cunyie*; *feign, feinyie*; the Norman French *campioun* in Blind Harry's *Wallace* for English and Central French *champion*; Scots *kinch* for English *chance*. On the other hand we have Scots *chanoun* for English *canon*, *roche* for *rock*, *sybow* for *chibol*, *moyen* for *mean(s)*, but *leal* for *loyal*.

There are, besides, some words which have not survived in Standard English but remain in English dialects or Scots, such as *ashet, aumrie, cowp* (to overturn), *douce, gean, groset, houlat, jigot, mavis, stank, tass(ie)*. All these are part of the common stock of French words that came to Britain, but Scotland received a further accretion from the Alliance made between John Baliol and the king of France in 1295, which lasted until the links with France were broken at the Reformation in 1560.

There has been a tendency to exaggerate the effect of the Auld Alliance on the vocabulary of Scots, and many words are ascribed to it which in fact came from the earlier periods of French influence in Scotland, but we can fairly safely credit it with the bulk of French words which are not found at all in English, Standard or dialect, such as *affeir* (pertain, be relevant), *disjune, jalouse, purpie, rew* (street), *vaig, bon-allie, Bon Accord, spairge*. The sixteenth century, when the Alliance was at its closest, gave us *aippleringie, dote* (endow), *fash, fiar, sussy, vivers, gardyloo, hogmanay, dams* (game of draughts), *bajan, howtowdie, caddie*, and the coins *hardhead* (<*hardit*, from Philippe le Hardi), *turner* (<*tournois* <*Tours*).

The last contributor to our vocabulary is Dutch or Flemish. The feudal kings encouraged the weaving industry in Scotland by importing the skilled craftsmen of Flanders and Brabant, who brought their Dutch with them; hence our two

Scots surnames Fleming and Brebner (<Brabander). Early
borrowings from Dutch include *cuit, craig* (neck), *crune,
bucht, coft* (bought), *dub, geck, golf, plack, redd* (tidy), *slap*
(gap), *wapinshaw, mutch, mutchkin, spiel* (climb), *loun*; later
came *callant, doit, howf, mows, kyte, pingle, plot* (scald),
skink, scone, lunt, fozie, pinkie, swack.

By the second half of the fourteenth century, French was
fading out of the picture; Gaelic was on the retreat from the
Lowlands (and there is evidence that even by 1200 it had
receded beyond Dunkeld and the foothills of Drumalban). The
language that was registering most progress was what the Earl
of March and others called *Inglis*, and by this northern name,
which serves to differentiate it somewhat from southern
English, it was known for the next three hundred years. It
made an impressive entry as a literary language in Barbour's
Brus, written in Aberdeen in 1375, in a translation or version
of parts of the *Golden Legend*, the stories of the saints, for
the benefit of those readers who found Latin difficult, and in a
translation of a long French romance about Alexander the
Great which the gentry could no longer read in the original. In
1390 Parliament began to record its business in Inglis instead
of Latin, and the old laws themselves were translated by
order of Parliament in 1425.

As regards nomenclature, Gaelic, which in Latin had been
hitherto called *lingua Scotica* (the language of the Scots, be it
noted, not the language of Scotland), had its name changed to
Hibernica or, in the lowland tongue, *Erse* or Irish; and in
1494 we find the national adjective *Scottis* applied for the first
time to what had now become the national tongue—the king
of Scotland's Scots as opposed to the king of England's
English. A considerable literature had sprung up in this
speech, not only in the poetry of alliterative verse, Blind
Harry's *Wallace*, Henryson and many popular anonymous
pieces, but also in prose, in translations of works from
French, Latin and even Danish. It was this business of
translation that threw up problems for writers of Scots; both
Gavin Douglas, who translated Virgil, and an unidentified
adaptor of a French work called *The Complaynt of Scotland*
(1548), stressed the need for borrowing to enlarge the
vocabulary and so increase the efficiency of the language.

The middle of the sixteenth century marks the beginning
of the end of Middle Scots and the emergence of Modern
Scots. The years 1460–1560 can be considered the heyday of

the Scots tongue as a full national language showing all the signs of a rapidly developing, all-purpose speech, as distinct from English as Portuguese from Spanish, Dutch from German, or Swedish from Danish. The Spanish ambassador at the court of James IV described the distinction as like that between Castilian and Aragonese. But in 1560 came the first great setback to Scots; the Reformation had the effect, politically, of swinging Scotland away from France into the Protestant and English camp, and, linguistically, of introducing literary English into every home in Scotland through the reading of the Bible. There was no Scots Bible available and the newest version ready for use was the translation made by English Protestant refugees in Geneva. English became associated with what was solemn, formal and dignified, the Word of God itself, while Scots continued in use for the day-to-day, familiar, homely, emotional or comic, i.e. at a lower intellectual pitch. To put it in broad, simple terms, English gradually took over as the literary or written language of Scotland, while the local forms of speech, the dialects, continued as the spoken tongue. Somewhat similarly, in Germany Luther's Bible became the literary standard, displacing the speech of the local chancelleries, especially in the north where Platt-Deutsch was the native tongue.

The anglicising process was helped on by the spread of books in Tudor English and by the setting-up of printers from England and France in Edinburgh in the late 1500s. The next serious blow to the growth of Scots was the Union of the Crowns, the departure of the Scottish court to London and its consequent adoption of English speech. The king's own work in prose and verse shows continuous anglicising, and later Scots poets of the seventeenth century, like Alexander, Hume, Mure and Drummond, wrote standard southern English, although occasional rhymes betray their Scottish pronunciation. The same development can be traced in the public and private documents of the period 1600–1650. The Union of 1707 was the last act in the story. When the legislature removed to London, English became in effect the official language of the whole country for law, administration, education and church usage, spoken as well as written. Scots became more and more restricted in use and scope, having lost spiritual status at the Reformation, social status at the Union of the Crowns, and political status with the Parliamentary Union.

Gaelic, as we saw, had taken to the hills in the fifteenth century and, with the fall of the semi-independent Lordship of the Isles, the feudal system gradually replaced the older clan system. With it came a penetration of Lowland interest and speech into the Highlands under the administration of James VI. Scots words appeared in the Gaelic vocabulary, like *bonnach* (bannock), *bùrn* (running water), *briogais, truibhse, tasdan, gartan, gairdean, pìob, cuidheall, breabadair.* There was conversely a further intake of Gaelic words into Scots from the fifteenth century onwards, e.g. *coronach, clarsach, shenachie, banshee, clan, clachan, caber, crine, connach, sons(ie), ingle, cranreuch, slogan, capercaillie, ptarmigan, tocher, corrie, partan, raith, Beltane.*

There was obviously a good deal of bilingualism, especially among Gaelic speakers in the Highland border areas. The great anthology of early Gaelic heroic and popular poetry, the *Book of the Dean of Lismore* (1512–1532), is written in a phonetic script based on the pronunciation of Scots, which the compiler must have been familiar with. The separation from Ireland was widened by the Reformation, and the next hundred years mark the period of decline in the classical verse-forms of Ireland and the rise of local forms of Gaelic, especially in the lyric verse of the seventeenth century. The spoken language of Gaelic Scotland, of which there are traces in the Dean's book, had begun to diverge from that of Ireland in the thirteenth century, although classical Irish was still used in the first Gaelic book to be printed in Scotland, Bishop Carswell's translation of Knox's *Liturgy* (1567), and in the classical Irish Bible of John Kirk which was circulated in 1690. But this prose was already archaic and conventional.

The political pressures on the language continued. Under the so-called Statutes of Iona in 1609, the old bards of the heroic tradition were to be banished and the sons of the chiefs were to be educated in the Lowlands, as indeed some of them had been already. During the Jacobite period from 1688–1746, the government, first in Edinburgh and then in London, intensified its control over potential rebels through military occupation, estate management and extended education. One of the greatest of Gaelic poets, Alasdair Mac Mhaighstir Alasdair, who was also a schoolmaster, was the author of a Gaelic-English glossary (1741) intended to further the teaching of English in the Highlands. And English it was, in the narrower sense of the term, because Scots by this time was *déclassé* and statusless. Hence the Highlander has never spoken Scots and hardly recognises any distinction between it and English. His word *beurla*, originally of any speech, is applied indiscriminately to both.

The eighteenth century saw the disappearance of Scots as a full language (in which, incidentally, it differs from Gaelic, which continued a full tradition in prose as well as verse, dialectal though its status might be); not only its vocabulary and grammar, but also its pronunciation was displaced by English. Through the increased contacts between England and Scotland, many Scots were hearing the sound of southern English as well as seeing its appearance on the printed page, and they were becoming more aware of the distinctions in pitch, quality and stress accentuation of their vowels in particular. This experience seems to have been traumatic for the Scots; various attempts were made during the rest of the century to correct Scottish speech by elocution lessons, by making lists of Scotticisms to be avoided (David Hume made one such list), and by articles and pamphlets on phonetics—all part of the polishing and refining and standardising process of the Augustan movement.

On the other hand, throughout the seventeenth century popular culture kept faithful to the old tongue in ballads, folk-songs and tales, in proverbs and sayings, and in comic verse. The current state of the spoken language is often revealed in, for example, letters from the uneducated (including women), and verbatim accounts in local records, especially Kirk Session minutes and witch-trials.

Some of the more popular verse was collected and published about the time of the Union and later by Allan Ramsay, who wrote poems himself in the vernacular tradition of Scots, producing love-songs, poetical epistles, humorous tales, genre pieces and the like. This tradition was taken up again by poets in the North-East, in Edinburgh by Fergusson, and above all in Ayrshire by Burns, whose triumphant success brought back Scots as a poetic language and helped to restore in some measure the prestige it had lost in the 1600s. His imitators were legion.

Scots prose, however, was not seriously attempted any more. Scott, Galt, Susan Ferrier, Hogg and their successors in the novel restricted their Scots to dialogue between Scottish characters like Meg Merrilees, Dandie Dinmont, Cuddie Headrigg, Caleb Balderstone, Jeannie Deans, who all belonged to the lower ranks of society that still naturally spoke Scots in the eighteenth century. The narrative of the novels is invariably in English, with the exception of Galt who experimented with a kind of Scotticised English in his narrative.

The chief differences, therefore, between the literary Scots of Scotland of the sixteenth and that of the eighteenth century are that in the latter there is no prose of a serious, technical or philosophical nature; the language of poetry is on a more popular and colloquial level; the vocabulary is much more limited and personal, more realistic and hence more regional—as in the case of the North-East—and in consequence local dialects, hitherto rather unobtrusive in Scottish literature, come into prominence, all the more readily in the absence of a metropolitan standard and a national literary centre. A classic example of the difference in scope and status of Scots and English appears in Burns's *The Cotter's Saturday Night*. The descriptive, intimate domestic scene and action are in Scots, but when the Bible is brought out there is an almost unconscious sliding into English, implicitly embodying the historical association of the Bible in Scotland with English. The declamatory moralising at the end is in fine Augustan too, as one would expect.

This was the state of affairs with Scots in the nineteenth and early twentieth centuries also. Gaelic fared better. Poets continued to use it for religious poetry, satire and political pieces; some even imitated Burns. Prose, which was the great deficiency in Scots, was cultivated to good effect and kept going not least by the famous Norman MacLeod in *Caraid nan Gaidheal*, and by the various publications of An Comunn Gaidhealach, the body set up to preserve and encourage the use of the language in the 1870s. (Of course there had been Gaelic societies in existence for a century before that.) Scots had nothing of the kind till the formation of the Lallans Society, now the Scots Language Society, in 1972.

Amidst the political and social upheavals following the First World War, small nationalities re-emerged. All over Europe, in Czechoslovakia, Yugoslavia, the Baltic States, the Netherlands, and (earlier) in the Faeroes, Iceland and Norway, there were movements to re-establish minority languages—a movement now extending to Brittany, Friesland, the Basque country, Israel, India and Africa. And Scotland has not remained unaffected in this. C M Grieve in the 1920s was talking of the restoration of a full canon of Scots—'back to Dunbar'—and writing some remarkably good poetry of a more intellectual content to back up his case. During the Second World War the 'Lallans' movement came to the fore with a new race of poets—William Soutar, Sydney Goodsir Smith, Robert Garioch, Douglas Young and others—and playwrights like Robert McLellan and Robert Kemp. Simultaneously, there was a similar upsurge in Gaelic poetry, with Sorley MacLean, George Campbell Hay, and later, Iain Crichton Smith and Derick Thomson. From a literary point of view the prospect now looks livelier than for a long time.

Many more people speak Scots than Gaelic, even more understand it; on the other hand, because of its kinship and similarity to English, Scots is becoming more and more confused with it and corrupted by it, and so fewer people speak it correctly, perhaps fewer than Gaelic. Gaelic still has the full canon and can be used for all purposes, prose as well as verse, whereas, as we have seen, Scots has been defective in prose since the seventeenth century. For instance, it is still possible to conduct a religious service or make a political speech entirely in Gaelic; to do this in Scots, where the tradition and models have both been lost, would be much more difficult, if not impossible.

Such then is the linguistic story of Scotland. We have seen how political history, literature and language have all been closely tied up and have interacted. What the future holds for them, what role Scots and Gaelic may still play in Scotland today and what the educational system can do, is doing, and how much more it should do, we must continue to explore with all the seriousness we can. The matter is too urgent to be postponed any longer.

2
Gaelic: its range of uses

Derick S Thomson

It is because Scotland's languages are in a state of flux that this book has been written. Not that being in a state of flux is an alarming, or even an unusual matter for languages. It might indeed be regarded as the normal healthy state, but though we can detect some high colour here and there in Scotland's languages, we may suspect that a canker is at work elsewhere. We are considering these matters now because the position of Scotland's languages is liable to change significantly and perhaps rapidly, and we think that there may be ways of directing or influencing that change. There are certainly opportunities for observing it, if we wish to confine ourselves to that academic purpose.

Although I must largely confine myself to the Gaelic situation, I cannot describe that accurately without being aware of other factors. I cannot analyse the range of uses of Gaelic without taking full account of the position of English in particular, and any look into the future—even the immediate future—will have its perspective determined by judgments of political probabilities for example. The farthest we can get with that kind of projection is to say: 'If such and such a situation obtains we may have x, y and z options.' I believe, however, that even this limited kind of projection may be worth making, because what we are doing in this whole exercise is attempting to crystallise basic attitudes and, if we succeed in that, beginning to form views and policies that may turn into practical politics five or ten or fifteen years hence.

I can most usefully begin by describing the position of Gaelic at the present time, in statistical, geographical and political terms. I shall then go on to discuss its range of uses, branching out from there into suggestion and prediction, in such a way (I hope) as will make it clear what is fact and what is projection.

Our main source of statistical information about Gaelic-speaking is the Census returns, and these now give as a bonus some information about the distribution of ability to read and write Gaelic. To some extent these statistics need to be interpreted in the light of what is mainly a subjective understanding of the situation. The 1971 Census returns, in brief summary, tell us that there were 88 892 Gaelic speakers in Scotland, an increase since 1961 of 7914 or approximately 9.8 per cent. Of these, approximately 48 000 were in the Highland counties (Argyll, Inverness, Ross and Cromarty and Sutherland), and of these 48 000, some 23 205 were in the Western (Outer) Isles, and of these 23 205, a total of 15 600 were in Lewis. These figures show us that the main area of Gaelic speech is the Outer Isles, and that by far the strongest community is in Lewis. But there are other figures of considerable interest. There were over 12 000 Gaelic speakers in Glasgow City, and in what is described as the Remainder of Scotland (i.e. all Scotland apart from the Highland Counties, Nairn, Bute, Perthshire and Glasgow) there were 25 185 Gaelic speakers, i.e. clearly more than a quarter of the total.

The areas with the highest percentage of Gaelic speakers are the following: Lewis Landward 89.5, North Uist 89.2, Harris 88.8, Barra 87.3, South Uist 77.2, Skye 66.9, Tiree and Coll 66.7, Stornoway 53.7, Islay 51.2, Lochcarron 50.7. The largest concentrations of Gaelic speakers in towns are (after Glasgow): Edinburgh 3340, Stornoway 2625, Inverness 2245, Aberdeen 1240, Oban 1025, Dundee 830, Paisley 630, Greenock 615 and Fort William 550. Elsewhere in Scotland there are a few areas of Gaelic strength, such as Sutherland, Ardnamurchan and parts of Wester Ross, but in the great majority of Lowland towns and districts the percentage of Gaelic speakers is very small, well below the average of 1.7 for the country as a whole. It is clear that there is now a settled pattern of general interest in Gaelic in non-Gaelic Scotland, and that this is what was beginning to show in the increase of Gaelic speakers in the 1971 Census; this increase was mainly in the Lowlands. The highest percentage areas show on paper little sign of decline, but the strength of the language among schoolchildren is clearly declining.

If we attempt to summarise the areas of activity most obviously associated with Gaelic, we find at once that this cannot be done on the same level for the whole of the Gaelic community. For example, it is only in the areas of main strength that Gaelic is a natural ingredient in the school curriculum, whether as a specific subject or as a medium of instruction. Its rôle as a medium of instruction varies enormously according to the educational administrative area, and within that according to the views and practices of headmasters and teachers. Thus Gaelic is most warmly encouraged within the school system in the Western Isles Region, but even here there is a wide spectrum of attitudes and practices. In Glasgow, by contrast, Gaelic is offered in three senior schools (and this number itself is in danger of being cut) and a little lip-service is paid to it in a few primary schools, but it is peripheral to the work of the schools and is sometimes taught outside school hours. To take another instance, the Gaelic church may either be the natural community church, as in many Highland areas, or a ghetto church, as in the cities and Lowland towns. The same kind of contrast applies in secular entertainment. Again, the range of uses of Gaelic will vary according to the educational backgrounds of the groups concerned.

We can take the analysis a step forward by considering the range of professional and other activities that have a direct link with the use of Gaelic, and the first thing that strikes one is how small that range is. The educational professions have perhaps the largest stake in Gaelic, and it is relevant to the work of teachers in schools, further education colleges, Colleges of Education and the universities. One Inspector of Schools has a Gaelic concern (as compared to three some twenty years ago), and there are two posts for Gaelic Advisers. It may happen that other educational administrators have a Gaelic involvement, but this will be more or less accidental. In the churches, Gaelic is still important in the smaller churches which have a strong Gaelic Area base, i.e. the Free Church and the Free Presbyterian Church. Its importance seems to grow steadily less in the Church of Scotland and it is peripheral in the Catholic and Episcopal Churches. In the media, Gaelic is strongest in radio; it has a foothold in television, in the press and in periodicals. There is a small but vigorous Gaelic publishing division and Gaelic has a small foothold elsewhere in publishing, but this whole sector is not large enough to provide more than office jobs for people with Gaelic qualifications. Professional language promotion accounts for a handful of posts in An Comunn Gaidhealach and in the Gaelic Books Council. It is common to find Gaelic speakers in nursing and social service posts in the Gaelic Area, but this is in no way mandatory. Similarly, local government services will often be run by local people who are Gaelic-speaking but the system they run is based on English documentation, and of course its official guidelines, in terms of circulars, regulations and legislation, are all in English. The Civil Service makes no Gaelic requirement of those it posts to Gaelic areas; indeed Gaelic was withdrawn from the list of Civil Service examination subjects some twenty years ago. The youth services, oddly enough, have no Gaelic wing. Law and accountancy have virtually no Gaelic links; industry and commerce have very few and virtually none in terms of official paper-work. In the whole range of Civil Service, local government, law, commerce and industry, the comparison with the position of Scots is quite close, but it will readily be seen that the positions of the two languages differ considerably in the other sectors discussed above.

The patterns of Gaelic's distribution—geographical and sociological—exert some influence on the range of uses that are open to it, or at least readily accessible in practical terms. We have to consider the concentration in the west and the thin but wide spread over the rest of Scotland. This points towards both an all-Scotland radio service and a booster Gaelic Area service, but there is still much argument about the place of Gaelic in the educational services. The concentration in the west boosts the place of Gaelic in the educational services (and in justice should boost it further), and by definition this requires a range of Gaelic use in higher education contexts and in administration. It should also imply a stronger Gaelic presence in the Scottish Education Department, but that logic has so far escaped attention. The concentration in the Outer Isles (the new Western Isles Region) should long ago have led to development of Gaelic as an official language in local government, but there are tentative moves in that direction now. Neither in education nor in government service is there a secure career structure linked to Gaelic, though there are the makings of one in education.

The fact that the strongest Gaelic areas are rural rather than urban produces another kind of imbalance and tension, and helps in turn to explain the lower status of Gaelic in legal, accounting, commercial and industrial contexts—all associated with towns and cities.

On the other hand Gaelic has a reasonably even spread across sociological groups. It is not a peasant language; this appears from its earlier history, and also from its recent literary standing. This gives the language more political weight than its mere numerical base would suggest.

The overall political weight is most important. It seems to me that this has not been much exploited yet, but it is there. Apart from the sociological and literary factors just mentioned, the historical position of Gaelic in Scotland makes a powerful intellectual and emotional claim, and acquires a strong symbolic significance, especially in a devolutionary, and *a fortiori* in an independence, context. The logic of this latter, and latter-day, situation suggests that ways should be found to satisfy a beneficial resurgence of the language. This resurgence should be beneficial in both the Scottish and the Gaelic Area contexts.

Already there are evidences of such a trend, for example the use of Gaelic on stamps and airmail letters and to some extent on public notices and signboards, the beginnings of such use in commercial situations, such as Gaelic cheque-books, *Gaelic* petrol, *Gaylick* soft drinks, *Glayva* liqueurs. Some of the *Gaelic* petrol-tankers carry (official) Gaelic phrases on their rear ends, and a number of firms use a little Gaelic in advertising. Gaelic on radio and television has a large non-Gaelic audience. But in government and official business, in road-signs, official literature of all kinds, the language has virtually no place.

In the Gaelic Area the position of Gaelic is naturally stronger, though it has no special position, indeed no position at all, in these 'national' areas which our centralised bureaucracy imposes on all alike. But Gaelic has some standing in the schools, in the Churches, in entertainment, in a few sectors of the public service, in commerce and industry (especially the fishing and tweed industries), in literature, and in local government. There is at least a sufficient base to build on. The building, however, needs both planning and sweat and toil.

Thus by a fairly lengthy and tortuous route I have come to the subject of my paper.

The range of uses of Gaelic in the current situation has already been suggested to some extent in these descriptive remarks. It may still be useful to give a short list of areas where the language is used and where it is dormant or underdeveloped. I shall now begin to use some specific examples and to discuss briefly the possibilities of development in particular areas of use.

Gaelic is used in a fairly wide range of literary modes: poetry (of various types), fiction, essays, biography, drama, children's literature, and in the reviewing of these forms of literature. This marks a salient difference between Gaelic and Scots at the present time. Most of these forms have a history of at least a hundred years, some of course much longer. But there is not much literary and musical criticism in Gaelic, and no art criticism. The literary critic is still at the stage of manufacturing technical terms, sometimes unnecessarily and simply because they are part of the stock-in-trade of English literary journalists. But though one might be dismissive of that kind of activity, it is true that literary criticism through the medium of Gaelic lacks a sufficiently flexible and precise technical vocabulary. Equivalents for *stream of consciousness, empathy, counterpoint, ambiguity,* even *symbol,* do not leap to mind. And so with musical criticism; a few years ago a short list of musical technical terms was published, and it has been used sparingly since then, but a great deal of this sort of development has still to take place. This sector, however, is not a source of worry—there is a fair variety, and a fair base for further development.

The use of Gaelic for the discussion of current affairs could be hugely extended. There is a certain amount in press and periodicals, and on radio and television, the main emphasis being on topics such as politics, local industry, local government; but there is little coverage of sport, hobbies, jazz, social services, foreign affairs. Each of these topics has its own technical vocabulary or jargon, or both, and all these modes of discourse would have to be developed, consciously and by practice. One of the serious drawbacks is of course the lack of motivated manpower. Market forces in a large society produce motivated manpower: it must be produced in a slightly different way in the Scottish, especially the Gaelic, context. There is, it is true, more than one possible answer. There might happen to come on the scene a Gaelic journalist with a mission to write about sport or the politics of Chile or China, though he would have to find a sympathetic editor, or perhaps an organisation could give cash inducements to some all-rounder to develop such interests. At the end of the day, the only sensible solution is to plan a selection of such developments, and give them a trial, an airing. It is one of the beauties of language that no such initiative is entirely wasted.

In the churches in the Gaelic Area, the language is used for sermons, extempore prayers, the general conducting of services, and local church business, and will be used to some degree in Sunday-school teaching, although the improbable bogey of examinations set in English inhibits this. But to the best of my knowledge Gaelic is little used in more general church business, at the level of Presbytery and 'above' in the Church of Scotland and the Free Church for example. Its use is almost completely at an oral level: it does not enter into office administration at all.

In education, Gaelic is of course used to some extent in examining and teaching at schools, colleges and universities, most consistently in recent years at Jordanhill College of Education. Its use could be much extended elsewhere. It is used very sparingly on the administrative level, one reason being that there is no recognised system of Gaelic shorthand (although there are *ad hoc* and personal adaptations) but even if there were, the chances of its being widely taught would not be good. However, such a system might possibly be brought into use in the Western Isles Region. Gaelic is not used much as a medium of instruction for other subjects in schools, and undoubtedly this would be the single most important step that could be taken now in the Gaelic educational field. For many years I have advocated the importance of this, and its merits have recently been argued in the book *Gaelic in Scotland* (ed D S Thomson, Gairm Publications, 1976). In the same week as that book was published there appeared a Gaelic textbook of biology (R MacLeoid, *Bith-èolas: A'Chealla, Ginntinneachd is Mean-fhàs* ed R Mac-Thómais, Gairm Publications, 1976) and this could act as an important test case. I shall return to the topic later, but it may be added here that a number of school subjects could well be taught through the medium of Gaelic, if adequate preparation were made. It is of course quite unfair to expect teachers used to English textbooks and teaching to change overnight to a different system. The way must be smoothed, for example by the provision of a suitable range of books, in-service courses, and so on.

It has already been suggested that the use of Gaelic in the Civil Service and in local government is minimal. It is used on cheques in the Western Isles Region, and no doubt a great deal in informal discussion. It may be used a little in certain committees, though the presence of a few English monoglots inhibits this, as it always does in the Scottish situation (it would not, for example, in a Welsh context). Western Isles Regional Councillors are perfectly ready to discuss Council topics in Gaelic on radio or television, so that it will be a relatively short step to transfer that fluency to the Council Chamber. This particular Council has ambitious plans for simultaneous translation and allowed for the appropriate fittings in its plans for new Council Chambers. When or whether it can afford this, and especially the staff to operate the service, is less clear. But other beginnings could be made. There could be bilingual minutes of committee and Council meetings. This would be a little cumbersome and inconvenient, but it would be a meaningful step to take, a demonstration of commitment.

It will be worth looking more closely at the implications of such a step, innocent as it may sound at first. The minutes of the Education Committee might present no large difficulties, and could perhaps be tackled simply by a reasonably competent translator or minute-taker, familiar with current Gaelic usage and concerned to produce a readable and faithful account of committee transactions. The problem of devising an appropriate register would be much less straightforward in the case of some other committee minutes, e.g. of discussions on town planning, sewerage, housing contracts or finance. There would undoubtedly be many decisions to be taken as to terminology and phraseology, and some of these would be quite complicated. The problem is not of course confined to such local government contexts. Essentially the same type of problem would arise in applying Gaelic to income tax regulations or schedules, licence forms (television, car), subsidy forms etc. Should one indulge in dreams of officialese that need not be turgid? Should one go so far as to think of a letter from the Tax Inspector that is a joy to read (for its style), or a television licence couched in felicitous phrases? It would in fact be rather exciting to start with a *tabula rasa* and train civil servants to write a spare, clear, elegant Gaelic for official purposes. The problem is not one of straightforward translation, but rather of honing down a piece of exposition, gaining maximum clarity and precision in small compass. The process also implies that certain words and phrases gain currency so that they can be used as a shorthand, as for example 'policyholder', 'commercial travelling' (used currently in a Certificate of Motor Insurance), or

'Schedule E' and 'personal allowances' (used in correspondence with the Inland Revenue).

A good case can be made for the provision in Gaelic of all the common forms which Gaelic citizens can normally be expected to deal with. It would be most economical, and most satisfactory from a methodological point of view, if a special unit could be set up to work out suitable forms of expression for such purposes, and also for the range of local government transactions. It would be a task of some complexity, needing the application of several minds, and needing quite extensive field testing, but for all that it should not be a lengthy task. Such a unit might be set up either at a university, or perhaps better, at a further education establishment (Lewis Castle College suggests itself as a possible base), but having some liaison with other bodies and individuals involved in relevant work.

Finally, I would like to return to the question of extending the range of subjects that might be taught through the medium of Gaelic. There is perhaps no need to rehearse the arguments for the desirability of doing this. Our concern for the moment is more with the broad range of a programme of this kind, its feasibility, and the nature of the problems involved. As to the range, it might be thought that history is a fairly obvious choice. In the early stages of school at any rate the emphasis on the narrative aspects of history should make for a painless transfer to the Gaelic medium; social and political history should not throw up too many linguistic problems; economic history on the other hand would need a good deal of linguistic spade-work before it was ready to be taught. Without minimising too much the problems of history teaching generally, this seems a project that could be tackled gradually, but soon, by the preparation of a series of textbooks which could be of a frankly derivative nature in some cases. A very small start has already been made with writing on geographical topics and this could be developed fairly easily; modern studies would be a natural follow-on.

There is a good deal to be said for teaching certain aspects of English, especially English literature, through the medium of Gaelic. There is of course another argument, that in a bilingual society English can well be taught through the medium of English, and no doubt this argument would be pressed more strongly than the one which seems to be entirely parallel to it, namely that Gaelic should be taught through the medium of Gaelic. For other foreign languages the sensible policy might be to use both English and Gaelic in their teaching. The most practical and likely development in this field is perhaps the publication of books in Gaelic on such topics. Already there is some experience of teaching music, biblical studies and certain aspects of technical subjects in some schools, and this could easily be extended. Mathematics, especially in its early stages, could be tackled, but this subject needs fairly expensive book publication if it is to be developed significantly.

Of the sciences, probably the life sciences and the descriptive sciences offer the best possibilities for Gaelic developments, but the difficulty is that these are not the most commonly taught in schools. Recently, however, as mentioned above, a Gaelic biology textbook has been published and it may serve as a case-study in several respects. The book was written in English by Dr Ranald MacLeod and was offered to me for translation and first publication in Gaelic. The numerous illustrations were professionally made under Dr MacLeod's supervision in the United States. The translation was tried out, in a preliminary way, by publishing some chapters in *Gairm*, but the book itself appeared in July 1976. Biology is not widely taught in schools, and has never been taught in Gaelic, so there is bound to be some hesitancy in introducing it. Fortunately the Nicolson Institute in Stornoway is going to try using it in their regular biology classes and presumably much can be learned from such an experiment. It remains to be seen how, and on what scale, such a textbook can be used elsewhere in the Gaelic school system; it may be anticipated that the Western Isles Region will be anxious to exploit the possibilities. The text has the advantage that it deals with such fascinating topics as the composition of the cell, genetics and the evolution of plant, animal and human life, the evolutionary chapters being especially well illustrated; thus the book has a deep general as well as textbook interest and could be used outside the science curriculum. However, the precarious nature of the venture can easily be appreciated. This would not matter too much for one textbook, but if a policy of extending the use of Gaelic is to have meaning it must be a continuing, expanding policy. The system as we have it could not stand the accumulation of a series of large deficits of finance and energy which would occur if such books were not put to adequate use. For example, work is already proceeding on a Gaelic biochemistry book which can build naturally on the diction of the Gaelic biology book, but will it be readily published or introduced into schools (and so, *a fortiori*, for possible books on botany, zoology, geology)?

And yet, in a way, I think I should apologise for harping so much on these practical difficulties, because such work is worth doing for its own sake, and for the sake of the challenge it gives to the language and to the writers and readers of the language.

In conclusion I would like to look more closely at the nature of this challenge, using the Gaelic biology book as an example. There was not, to my knowledge, any previous discussion in Gaelic of this subject-matter. The topic of evolution loomed menacingly on the Gaelic scene last century but this was in a theological context and did not involve much discussion of technical detail. There was therefore the initial problem of choosing, or making, a set of technical terms. Dr MacLeod provided some very useful spade-work here, by listing sets of European terms in many instances. On vocabulary items, the first decision in principle was whether the term should simply fall into line as an international, or at least common-European, technical term, or whether it had sufficient general application in a Gaelic context to justify a more Gaelic-based term. It was on this principle that an easily recognisable Gaelic-based term was chosen for *acid* (*searbhag*), *carbohydrate* (*gualuisg*), *genetic* (*ginteil*) and *organism* (*fàs-bheairt*), whereas an adaptation of an international term was chosen in more severely technical instances, as those of *amino acid* (*searbhag amino*), *chromosome* (*cromosom*), *gamete* (*gamait*), *hydrogen* (*haidrodean*), *protoplasm* (*protoplasma*), or *ultra-violet* (*ultra-violait*). Now I would not claim, nor wish to claim, that all the judgments of that kind were consistent, or inspired. It might be argued, for example, that *carbohydrate* (*gualuisg*) and *hydrogen* (*haidrodean*) should have been dealt with on the same principle, and that argument would be as meaningful as mine that *carbohydrate* is a more common concept than *hydrogen*. I tried to avoid putting one kind of consistency above common sense or practical expediency, and so in finding an equivalent for, say, *biochemical*, I was content to borrow the second half of the word but translate the first, arriving at *bith-cheimiceach*; or in the case of *photosynthesis* to borrow the first element but translate the second, giving *foto-cho-chur*. On the other hand I was often drawn to a non-hybrid solution, as for example in the series *cell* (*cealla*, which simply adapts semantically an existing Gaelic word), *unicellular* (*aoncheallach*), *multicellular* (*ioma-cheallach*). Another attractive kind of solution lay in the interpretative coinage that uses a metaphor to carry conviction or hasten understanding, as *enzyme* which was translated *beirmeir*, from *beirm* (yeast). Conversely, faced with as foreign a pair of words as *eukaryotic* and *prokaryotic*, with their mixture of classical and English elements, I resorted to rather wooden translations (*fìor-chnòthach* and *roimh-chnòthach*) fearing that no degree of ingenuity known to me would allow that pair to carry their meanings in their faces. I must admit also that there was an element of leg-pulling (which did not altogether fail in its intention) in the equivalent for *deoxyribonucleic acid* (DNA), which in Gaelic became *searbhag deocsairioboniuclasach* (SDN). This must have a strong claim to be the longest, or at least the most awkward, word in Gaelic. When I discovered that there had been five different translations used in the book for *complex* (*co-thoinnte, eadar-fhillte, eadar-thoinnte, iomadh-fhillte* and *casta*) I let the five stand!

The complexities of coinage and translation are only the first order or layer of complexities; those that arise in weaving that vocabulary into continuous exposition are equally challenging and fascinating for the writer. But enough is enough for one essay and I leave that subject, merely saying that it seems to me that both processes (word-making and word-weaving) are best tackled in harness—that is the most creative way of tackling such a problem, and the one most likely to carry conviction in the end. While I do not propose to translate another scientific textbook myself, I commend the exercise with enthusiasm to other people!

3
Scots: its range of uses

J Derrick McClure

At first sight, the task of examining the range of uses of Scots would appear to be fairly straightforward. Scots is extensively used in both speech and writing; and it is common knowledge that for certain types of literature (e.g. poetry) its use is well-established, whereas for other types (e.g. scientific treatises) it is virtually or completely non-existent. All that requires to be done, therefore, is to ascertain which of the stylistic registers available in a fully-developed literary language are present in Scots, and which are missing; what effects can be gained, and what effects cannot be, or at any rate have not been, gained by means of writing in Scots.

There is, however, a difficulty at the very outset, a difficulty which does not arise in a similar discussion of Gaelic. In Gaelic we have a language which is instantly identifiable. It is highly distinctive, readily distinguishable even from its nearest relative (Irish), and certainly bearing no obvious resemblance to either Scots or English. Its speakers are for the most part full bilinguals who use Gaelic in some situations and English in others, making a clear and unmistakable distinction between the two. Admittedly, many Gaelic speakers—especially young speakers—employ English loan-words on a fairly extensive scale, even where appropriate Gaelic words exist; and in literary usage we find partial hybrids such as the anglicised Gaelic of Iain Crichton Smith and the Gaelicised English of Fionn Mac Colla. In principle, however, it is nonetheless true that the two languages are, at least potentially, wholly distinct and mutually independent.

In the case of Scots, by contrast, the situation is not nearly so clear-cut. However adulterated the Gaelic language may be in practice, the theoretical concept of Gaelic is well-defined. No such clarity exists in the concept of Scots: it is, on the contrary, extremely nebulous. It could easily be a matter for debate whether a given speaker was talking Scots or not, or whether a certain piece of writing was in Scots or not. In the first place, Scots and English are very closely related. Of course, comparisons made from a dialectologist's standpoint show obvious and striking differences, but on a wider view Scots and English are similar. In terms of comparative philology English and Dutch could be described as similar, and Scots is obviously more like English than is Dutch. It is, in fact, a familiar point of controversy whether Scots ought to be classed as a distinct language at all: my view is that it cannot justifiably be described as a dialect of English, which conveys the misleading impression that Scots is derived from *modern* English and thus demotes it to the status of, say the speech of Harlem, New York. However, I would regard it as acceptable to class Scots and English together as dialects of *Anglic* (using that word as a cover-term to include the language of the Anglo-Saxon invaders of the fifth century and all the speech-forms derived from it).

Not only have Scots and English always been, relatively speaking, similar, but for a long time, and especially in the last hundred years, the linguistic influences of Standard English, including specifically *English* English, have been operating strongly on Scots, with the result that many of its distinguishing features have been, or are being, lost. The effect of this is that the Lowlands, like the Highlands, is still largely a bilingual region; but whereas in the Gàidhealtachd the situation is theoretically comparable to that of Belgium or Quebec, with two distinct languages being used on an 'either-or' basis, in the Lowlands bilingualism operates rather on a basis of 'more-less'. Relatively few people speak unequivocal Scots on some occasions and unequivocal English on others (though this does occur, in areas such as the North-East where the local form of Scots is both well-preserved and highly differentiated—I have found it, for example, in Aberdeen University students). The much commoner situation is that the language of a given individual will sometimes contain a greater and sometimes a lesser number of Scots forms. The question immediately arises, therefore, of where Scots ends and English begins. *I'll not be going home till eleven o'clock tonight* is obviously English; *A'll no be gaun hame ti aleevin a'cloak the nicht* is obviously Scots, and both are perfectly possible utterances. But what about *I'll no be going home till eleven o'clock the night, I'll no be gaun home ti eleven a'cloak the night*, or any of several other equally possible permutations of the Scots and English forms?

Nor is this the only difficulty. A Peterhead fisherman and

a Selkirkshire farmer might readily be said to speak Scots; and although their vocabulary, idiom and pronunciation will differ considerably, this does not present a serious problem of definition: all languages, of course, have different dialects. But what about a Glasgow docker? His idiolect, unlike those of the fisherman and the farmer, would probably contain very few Scots words: the distinctive vocabulary of Scots has largely disappeared in the cities. He might not even use Scots phonological forms: he would be more likely to say *home* than *hame, make* than *mak, find* than *fin.* Yet his speech would be very unlike that of a teacher or a doctor from the same city; and to a professional man from, say, San Francisco it would certainly present serious problems of intelligibility. Is the docker speaking Scots? By definition, differences of pronunciation alone are not sufficient grounds for classifying two speech forms as separate dialects, let alone separate languages, and it would be mostly pronunciation features that would constitute the regional and social markers in his speech; yet the differences between his idiolect and that of our San Francisco man would be so considerable that it would sound strange to say that they were both speaking Standard English—even with different accents. The same question could arise with reference to the literary language. Flora Garry could be said to write in Scots, and so could Tom Leonard; but if 'Scots' covers the languages of both those poets, it must be a decidedly fluid term.

A further point is that both Flora Garry and Tom Leonard, though their styles are vastly different, write in forms that are recognisably based on some people's actual speech. But what about writers like Sydney Goodsir Smith or Alexander Scott, whose Scots often contains words that are probably no longer to be found in anybody's conversational vocabulary: words, moreover, which even when they were in active use were to be heard in widely separated areas of the country and could never have existed together in the speech of any individual? MacDiarmid's *Sangschaw* and *Penny Wheep,* for example, contain several words from his own Border dialect—*hanlawhile, switchable, scoogie, guissay, bobquaw, danders*—but they also contain words that originate from the North and North-East: *blinter, tyauve, ablach, swippert, haingles.* Is this literary 'synthetic' Scots as much, or more, or less, Scots than the Scots of the dialect writers? Certainly it is a different kind of Scots, and a different sense for the word.

In fact, it simply does not suffice to say that a particular piece of speech or writing is 'in Scots': the term is too ill-defined. We cannot begin to discuss the range of uses of Scots before finding some scheme which will make the word unambiguous.

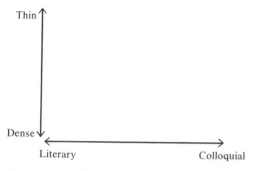

Figure 3:1

Figure 3:1 may assist in clarifying the issue. On the horizontal or X-axis of the chart, a piece of writing would be placed near the 'colloquial' end if it approximated closely to actual speech: if it contained only such words and idioms as some people do in fact use in conversation, or if it employed an orthography that suggested a definite and readily identifiable mode of pronunciation. 'Colloquial' writing might employ slang or jargon, and might attempt to suggest the lack of overt attention to formal grammatical rules that characterises spoken language. It would not abound in rhyme, alliteration, syntactic parallelisms, metaphors, or any other obviously 'poetic' features. To the extent that those were present, the passage would be moved away from the 'colloquial' and towards the 'literary' end of the scale. 'Literary' Scots, by contrast, is by definition remote from actual speech. Some of its characteristics would be: a more or less recondite vocabulary, containing words from a wider range of times and places than could be found in 'colloquial' writing; an avoidance of distinctively local forms in grammar and orthography (a literary writer might prefer *he's no coman* and *they dinna* to *he's nae coman* and *they dinnae* as the latter pair are more regionally marked; and he might use the spelling *guid*, which can suggest several different pronunciations equally well, rather than *gweed*, which can suggest only one); and of course, the presence in some degree of figurative and allusive language and formal versification. (Note that the degree of literariness does not depend solely on the degree of Scotsness.)

The vertical or Y-axis of the chart is labelled at one end 'thin' and at the other end 'dense'. 'Thin' and 'dense' Scots are defined by their degree of differentiation from Standard English. It should be emphasised that this is merely for descriptive convenience and has no further significance. It does not imply, for example, that Scots is in any real sense a deviation from a standard represented by English. The reason for taking Standard English as the norm for comparison is simply that it is well-defined, incontrovertibly recognisable, and—alas—for all of us nowadays, the first and in many cases the only language which we ever learn to read and write. To the extent that a piece of Scots writing is unlike English, it tends towards the 'dense' end of the scale. (Though the definition is in a sense negative this too should not be misunderstood: it is, of course, not an absence of English features that entitles a sample of language to be classed as Scots, but the positive presence of Scots ones.) If the piece contains a large number of distinctively Scots words, if it is Scots in grammar and idiom, if it is written in an orthography that is clearly based on Scots pronunciation or Scots etymology, then it is a sample of 'dense' Scots. Conversely, if only relatively few of its words and other features are distinctively Scots, it would be placed near the 'thin' end of the axis.

The limiting case, as it were, of 'thin' Scots would be Scottish English, i.e. Standard English, the international *lingua franca*, as spoken by educated Scotsmen. This is fairly readily identifiable, and not only by features of pronunciation: it has characteristic words and idioms as well. The boundary between Scots and Scottish English is not entirely clear-cut, and in some cases it might be debatable whether a given word or idiom belongs to one dialect or to the other. However, it would presumably be agreed that when we gather *brambles* or *rowans*, *jag* ourselves on *whins*, attend a public *roup*, catch a *parr* in a *burn* in *spate*, observe that the windows are *needing washed*, ask *what age* a child is and learn that he is *four past in August*, say *we'll away* to the common-room to *wait on* a friend, or use *next Thursday* to mean Thursday of next week even if we say it on Monday, we are not, by virtue of those usages, speaking Scots. Many people who would vigorously reject the notion that they spoke Scots at all would use forms like those as a complete matter of course. They are speaking English just as an American is speaking English when he walks along the *sidewalk* to the *movie-theater* and stops on the way to have a *soda-pop* at the *drugstore*.

Scottish English is not in itself Scots. It is one of the local forms of English, characterised like all the other local forms by features of vocabulary, idiom, and (of course) pronunciation. If the Y-axis were protracted upwards beyond the point represented by Scottish English, it would lead in the direction of a non-regional English. This concept could be meaningful only when applied to the written language: there is no such thing as non-regional *spoken* English, for every speaker has at the very least a regional accent. However, a short article in a respectable newspaper, for example, would probably contain in its language no evidence whatever of its district or even country of origin. Where an upward prolongation of the Y-axis would *not* lead would be to the Standard English of England. That could be positioned relative to the present chart, if at all, only by adding a third dimension: it would be represented by a point at the same level as Scottish English but 'outwards' from the chart, along a Z-axis at right angles to the other two. This is true for the simple reason that English Standard English is just as much a local form as Scottish Standard English: 'Do come in, that's right . . . I expect you'd like to go straight up, wouldn't you?'[1] is as regionally marked as 'More likely he was down to take a bit keek at you, Chris lass',[2] or, for that matter, 'Huh, we ain't got no two bits. Where you 'spec we gonna get us two bits?'[3]

The chart is, of course, an oversimplification: it completely ignores the time dimension, for example. If this were introduced, complications would immediately occur. The dialogue of William Alexander's *Johnny Gibb of Gushetneuk* would clearly be placed near the 'colloquial' end of the scale. When that book was written there were still large numbers of people who spoke as 'Gushets' and his friends are represented as speaking; and the dialogue is a deliberate attempt to reproduce their speech. The dialogue of W P Milne's *Eppie Elrick* is in many respects very similar, yet it would have to be classed as much more 'literary'; on the grounds that in the 1950s, when *Eppie* was composed, it would have been difficult or impossible to find anybody who could speak such pure North-East Scots, and maintain it with absolute consistency through such lengthy monologues, as do the characters in that book. Their dialogue is not a reproduction of actual speech but a historical reconstruction of an obsolescent speech form, and is therefore in a different stylistic category. To avoid such complications, the chart would have to be defined as being a viable mode of description only for literature produced within a fairly narrowly limited time span.

Some specific illustrations of different areas of the chart may now be examined.

1 'Thin literary'

> Howkit frae some howe in France, thir banes
> Lig here the day in this pregnant shrine
> Heich abuin Embro's traffic, on the Castle cleuch:
> A sacrifice uphauden til our auld god Mars
> By the pagan worshippers doun there i' the toun.
>
> Wha's aucht him? Whit man and woman felt
> In their bed o love or simple human affection
> The bairn he wes kick at the wame-waa?
> Wes he Ours or Theirs? Did he speik the leid
> That I speik? Or did the Cockney slang
> Ping like bullets frae his lips? Or did
> The tongue o Hölderlin, or Baudelaire
> Inform the constitution o his body-saul?
>
> Nae maitter. He is Ours and Theirs, he is Man
> Suicidit by his ain ill-will, the tongue
> He speiks nou is the human tongue that says
> The same in Swahili, Japanese or Scots,
> And whit it says nae humans need translatit.

Tom Scott, *At the Shrine o the Unkent Sodger*

In Tom Scott's long philosophical poem, the language is clearly Scots, or at least contains Scots elements. This short extract shows Scots features of phonology (*heich, auld, doun, whit, nae maitter*), grammar (*thir, uphauden, til, wha's aucht*), and vocabulary (*howk, howe, lig, cleuch, wame, leid*). Throughout the poem, forms such as these occur fairly consistently. On the other hand, several phrases, lines, and even longer sections have nothing or virtually nothing Scots about them: philosophical concepts or ordinary abstractions, for example, are invariably expressed by means of English words. In the present extract *this pregnant shrine* and *simple human affection* are obvious cases, and elsewhere in the poem we find *lunatic destruction, competitive private greed, social co-operation, God's creation revealed in a kingfisher's flash, War is Profit escaped frae the Zoo's ape-house/ And at large among men, like a killer gorilla, . . . the Higher Apes/That sit in government office, or rin a lab,/Are utterly unfit to mak moral decisions.* Except for a few details which could be altered with very little difference to the overall effect, there is nothing in the language of such passages to show that they are the work of a Scottish writer. In fact, the proportion of Scots forms in this poem is, comparatively speaking, not high. It must therefore be placed near the top or 'thin' end of the upright axis.

The Scots features themselves include a large number of very common and well-known Scots words: *howe, lig, abuin, bairn, wame, cheil, skail, darg, thole* and many others. However, they also include some extremely rare and obscure words: *torkit* (tortured), *sparple* (scattering), *shent* (shamed), *smool* (scowl), *forfairn* (exhausted), *spreital* (spiritual). Frequently, Scots is used for a clearly-marked poetic effect: the first line of the poem is an instance, with the assonance on *howkit and howe,* and other excellent examples are *Gane as the wind lifts a sparple o sand, The sea-maws keenan your waes by your lang, lane shores, A pentit savage fits til his stentit bow/A strategic weapon, Flodden a wheen sangs and a mood o keenin.* Clearly, this is 'literary' and not 'colloquial'. In this poem, Scott is using a language which consistently keeps at least a foothold in Scots and often uses Scots forms with impressive poetic force, but which modulates easily to literary English when the argument can be expressed with equal vigour and clarity through the medium of that language.

    2   'Dense literary'

> But geyan gash she lours in a gurlie gloamin
> Whan seipan swaws are graveyaird gray on the strand,
> The hills as dreich as deid lichen,
> The dowie rivers drounan the dark lift,
> The toun a cauldrife cairn o tauchie rock
> Mair steel nor stane, the streets in snell canyons
> Trenchan through craigie scaurs that sklaff the sun,

A wersh warld, its colours aa wan-blae,
Whaur lugs are deaved by the drantan dirge o the sea
And een blunted on drumlie blads o granite.

Alexander Scott, *Heart of Stone*

In marked contrast to the style of the preceding extract is that of Alexander Scott's poetic description of Aberdeen. Whereas in Tom Scott's poem the proportion of Scots to English vocabulary items is relatively low, in Alex Scott's nearly every word is distinctively Scots. This is not entirely true of the grammar: the English *-ed* ending of the past participle is used instead of the Scots *-it*, and plural subjects take the verb *are* although the Scots usage would, strictly, be *is*. (This feature might be seen as more appropriate to a 'colloquial' than to a 'literary' register; but the association is due simply to Standard English influence and is an unnecessary one.) Some grammatical features, however, are clearly Scots, such as the present participle in *-an* and verbal noun in *-in*, the plural *een, mair . . . nor*.

Obviously this is 'dense' Scots: as far as the vocabulary is concerned, almost maximally dense. It is also immediately recognisable as 'literary' rather than 'colloquial'. Many of the words are common currency: *geyan, lour, gloamin, dreich, lift, snell, wersh, lug, deave*, and at least two in the present extract have a decidedly North-East ring: *seipan* and *sklaff*. Others are now rare or poetic: *gash, gurlie, swaws, tauchie, drant*. More important, however, is the striking use of traditional literary devices: hyperbole (lines 4 and 7), simile (lines 2 and 3), and, most prominent of all, the strongly rhythmic swing of the lines and the forceful and pervasive alliteration and assonance. The words have clearly been chosen not only for their meaning but very decidedly for their sound as well. Technical skill of this kind (*note* kind, not degree) would not be exemplified in writing at the 'colloquial' end of the scale.

3 'Thin colloquial'

Clydebridge . . .
sprawled oot
yet strauchlin to the lift
wi cranes
and steel-waad sheds.

And yet croodit into
the bend o the river
Clyde.
We pass at speed
on the Mid-Day Scot
traivellin back or furrit.

I hae great feelin
for the place
peerin oot the windae.
You micht say it is *my*
place. I hae sent doon
roots
for aa the times I've been
uprootit
yet there's thae wee white anes
that feed my mind
and mak reality
in the imagination.

I canna claim
to ken the warks.
A regular passenger
could hae seen
wi guid een
mair than me.
An 'O' level student
ken mair o steel-
makin.
I've ne'er e'en got by the gates
earned ane penny piece
(auld or new)
or raised ane drap o sweit
frae steel.
And yet thae warks
are in my bluid
and banes.

I'm agin their pride
in wark;
agin the haurd men
and e'en the raw reid
Clydeside. I'm for free men
and dinna ken the pride

in haurd manual wark
—'no haein the need o it'
they can richtly say.
Nae doot the present
inhabitants o Clydebridge
would reject me
(aa but ane or twa relatit to me)
but that is their richt
or their ignorance
o the strength
o wee white roots
e'en when broken aff.

Duncan Glen, *A Journey Past*

The language of Glen's poem-sequence would be placed almost as far away as possible on the chart from that of *Heart of Stone*. The style is much more suggestive of conversational speech that that of either of the two poems previously considered. The informal, indeed formless, *vers libre*, intended to suggest the internal monologue of a man thinking to himself during a train journey through industrial Clydeside, conveys something of the loose organisation of real speech. Colloquial idioms are frequent: *traivellin back or furrit, peerin oot the windae, no haein the need o it,* and elsewhere in the poem *needin quiet to get his sleep, an him deid afore I was born.* At first sight there are a fair number of Scots forms, and certainly Scots phonology is frequently instanced: *oot, waa, haurd, windae, drap, banes.* Perhaps, indeed, this aspect of the language is if anything somewhat 'denser' than the persona of the poem might in real life be expected to use. On the other hand, there are several English features for which the Scots equivalents could have been substituted without the result seeming artificial: *I've, would, mair than, thae warks are.* Scots vocabulary items, too, are relatively rare: *strauchle* is the only example in this extract. Some occur in the rest of the poem, for example *baggies, sclim, guddle, clairt, braw, kye, bing* and *tyaav,* but the list is not long. All of these are certainly still in active use, although whether a Glasgow man would be likely to say *kye* or *tyaav* is open to question. On the whole, the language of this passage would have to be placed near the 'thin' end of the scale, and certainly it is 'colloquial' rather than 'literary'.

4   'Dense colloquial'

Haw, the George Squerr stchumers huv pit the hems
oan Toonheid's answer tae London's Thames;
thuv peyed a squaad ooty Springburn broo
tae kinfront the Kinawl wi its Watterloo,
an dampt up Monklan's purlin stream
fur some dampt bailie's petrol dream,
some Tory nutter wi caurs oan the brain—
jis shows ye, canny leave nuthin alane,
the scunners.

Stephen Mulrine, *Nostalgie*

The fourth basic type of written Scots, 'dense colloquial', can
be exemplified by an extract from one of Stephen Mulrine's
Glasgow poems. A striking feature of Mulrine's work in this
genre is his use of a phonetic orthography to indicate Glasgow pronunciation: *oan, ooty, squaad, kinawl, caur, Ah hud,
mibbe, fulla, thur.* This differentiates the language very considerably from Standard English, and therefore makes it
'dense'. Colloquial idioms abound, to a much greater extent
than in Glen's poem: in fact, whereas the latter suggests a
relatively unmarked language in which specifically Glasgow
turns of phrase are occasionally brought in to maintain the
identity of the persona within the supposed setting of the
poem, Mulrine's style is emphatically rooted throughout in
the typical phraseology of Glasgow speech. *Monklan's purlin
stream* is not necessarily an exception to this, as a working-
class Glaswegian could easily use such a phrase ironically:
the use for humorous or sarcastic effect of words or phrases
that would normally characterise a more elevated register is
typical of Western Urban patter, and is frequently represented in literature of the area. The dialogue in the novels of
the excellent Kilmarnock writer William MacIlvanney, for
example, abounds in specimens. (*Petrol dream*, however,
strikes me as rhyme-forced and unconvincing.) Phrases such
as *pit the hems oan* . . . , *jis shows ye, canny leave nuthin
alane*, or, from other verses of the poem, *a baw, ur a bike,
even* . . . *thull gie ye the jile*, and words like *stchumers, broo,
terrs, chuckies, wheech*, could be heard in any pub or back
green. Clearly, Mulrine is attempting with considerable success to give as accurate a reproduction as possible of a very
distinctive speech form. The passage has one element which

is obviously 'literary' and not 'colloquial': it scans and rhymes. In this respect it would have to be positioned slightly to the left of Glen's poem on the chart, as well as fairly far below it. However, the dominant impression is very clearly that of a colloquial register.

It is thus possible, at least theoretically possible, on this analysis, to position any given piece of Scots writing at some point on a chart of which the four corners, as it were, represent the polar extremes of thin literary, dense literary, thin colloquial and dense colloquial. None of the four passages discussed could be seen as an actual extreme case (although the Alex Scott extract, at least, comes very close to it), but they can clearly be distinguished from each other in terms of such a scheme. Of course, the categories shade into each other. The difference between thin and dense is a matter of degree. So, in a sense, is the difference between colloquial and literary, but the theoretical implications of this distinction are much greater. Colloquial Scots retains a close relationship with the spoken language; literary Scots does not. Scots as a vehicle for literature has cut loose from its moorings in a way that English, for example, has not done. The reason for this is straightforward; and, though the effects of it are perhaps more conspicuous now than ever before, the principle is by no means new.

Since the dying out of the great literature of Middle Scots, there has been no standard form for the Scots language: it has existed only as a group of dialects. Whereas a writer in English has a standard literary language ready made, a writer in Scots has had the choice of employing a local dialect which makes no pretensions to being a national language, or attempting to create a literary language of his own. Now, the first choice inescapably imposes a limitation: it is impossible to express the highest and most sublime thoughts in the everyday tongue of a group of people. If this appears to be an elitist stance, the fact requires no apology. It is true almost by definition that the capacity for experiencing real exaltation of thought and feeling *and* of conveying it in words is a capacity which very few people have. It follows that the sort of language which an ordinarily assorted group of people, such as the speakers of a given dialect, use and understand among themselves in their everyday activities cannot be used for the greatest of literature. This applies, note, to *any* dialect, whether or not it is the basis for a literary language.

An English-speaker who boasts that his language is superior
to all others because it is the language of Shakespeare has the
right to make that boast if, and only if, he makes the same use
of the English language as Shakespeare did: and in general,
most speakers of Standard English get as near to Shakespeare's range of expression as do most speakers of Glasgow
slum dialect. No poet (not even Wordsworth, despite his
theories) has expressed sublime thought in commonplace
language: it is simply not possible to do so. Of course, this
limitation is of absolutely no importance for most people.
Any spoken dialect is more than adequate to express all the
normal thoughts, feelings and emotions, and to describe all
the ordinary daily activities, of nearly all its speakers. When a
major writer has something to say which goes beyond that,
however, he must of necessity go beyond the range of a
spoken dialect. By restricting his literary language to such
words and idioms as people ordinarily use, a poet by no
means prohibits himself from writing good poetry; but he
prohibits himself from writing poetry of international calibre.
A Charles Murray, a Violet Jacob, or a T A Robertson
(*Vagaland*) can produce admirable work within the confines
of a local dialect; but a Fergusson, a Burns, a Scott (be he
Walter, Alex or Tom), or a MacDiarmid is both able and
obliged to overstep those confines in order to express all that
he wants to express.

This situation is neither new nor peculiarly Scottish: it is
universal. The Scottish sociolinguistic situation, however, has
resulted in its becoming exceptionally conspicuous here and
now. A language spoken naturally and for all purposes by all
sections of a culturally autonomous society is, barring a
catastrophe, self-renewing. If it is also the language of a
literate people, its spoken and written forms will exist in a
symbiotic and mutually beneficial relationship. This was the
case in late-medieval Scotland. Even in the eighteenth century, the spoken forms were still vigorous enough to provide
a solid foundation for the language of great poets. Nowadays
the situation is far from comparable. The Scots dialects are
spoken by only a section—and not the most socially prestigious section—of the community, they are for the most part
ignored by the mass media and discouraged by the educational system, and they appear only rarely and sporadically
in writing. (Certainly some progress is being made towards
rectifying this deplorable situation; but even if its momentum

can be maintained and increased, some time will have to pass before any major effect becomes visible.) Under such conditions a language cannot be expected to flourish. In the case of Scots, it is remarkable that it has survived even as well as it has; and it has unquestionably suffered a massive attrition of its active vocabulary and a progressive dilution of its distinctive grammatical and phonological features.

The corollary to this is that the limitations imposed by choosing to write in a Scots dialect are greater than ever, and that the necessity for a writer of major gifts to escape from the confines of a dialect will be more compelling than it was in the time of Burns. This, plus the absence of a standard national form of Scots, has had the apparently paradoxical effect of giving great freedom to Scots writers. If the range of expression afforded by any single Scots dialect today is relatively small (relative, that is, to what is required by a major poet, not to what is required by an ordinary man in his everyday life), the range of expression of the entire Scots language, past and present, is enormous. Because the contrast is so glaringly obvious, many contemporary Scots writers have opted for a frankly artificial language, constructed by selecting from Scots of different regions and periods; and by this means have achieved brilliant effects. We therefore have the superficially strange, but readily explicable, situation that although spoken Scots has never been weaker, Scots literature has never since the eighteenth century been stronger. This situation would not occur, or not so obviously, in a language of which the spoken form was fully established for all purposes. In the modern literature of England there is no register comparable to what we are calling dense literary Scots.

If the foregoing argument is accepted, it is predictable that the most important and the best work in modern Scots literature has been achieved through the medium of literary Scots. *Mutatis mutandis*, the same is true in any age. Very few writers of the first rank have tied themselves closely to a single dialect as the basis of their works. Galt and perhaps Soutar are the only possible exceptions known to me, and the writing of both of them is clearly 'literary' and not 'colloquial' in other respects. Even in the medieval period, although poems like *Kynd Kittok*, *The Wyf of Auchtermuchty*, and *Peblis to the Play* are in a sense more characteristically Scottish than poems like *Orpheus and Eurydices*, *The Gol-*

dyn Targe and *The Palace of Honour*, it is the poetry typified by the latter group that forms Scotland's most important contribution to the great medieval European literary tradition. However, though a colloquial, and particularly a dense colloquial, style prohibits major literature, it by no means prohibits literature which within its limitations is very good. Many writers elect to use dense colloquial Scots for their work, and a fairly wide range of effects is possible within it. It is therefore appropriate, since the emphasis so far has been on the restrictions imposed by a colloquial register, to conclude by examining some illustrations of the considerable variety which it allows.

> It wis jist a skelp o the muckle furth,
> A sklyter o roch grun,
> Fin granfadder's fadder bruke it in
> Fae the hedder an the funn.
> Granfadder sklatit barn an byre,
> Brocht water to the closs,
> Pat fail-dykes ben the bare brae face
> An a cairt road tull the moss.

> Bit wir fadder sottert i the yard
> An skeppit amo' bees
> An keepit fancy dyeuks an doos
> 'At warna muckle eese.
> He bocht aul' wizzent horse an kye
> An scrimpit muck an seed;
> Syne, clocherin wi a craichly hoast,
> He dwine't awa, an deed.

> I look far ower by Ythanside
> To Fyvie's laich, lythe lan's,
> To Auchterless an Bennachie
> An the mist-blue Grampians.
> Sair't o the hull o Bennygoak
> An scunnert o the ferm,
> Gin I bit daar't, gin I bit daar't,
> I'd flit the comin' term.

> Flora Garry, *Bennygoak*

Perhaps the simplest use of the colloquial register is for frankly local poetry: poems written specifically for the people of a particular community, often with that community's distinctive way of life as their subject matter. A writer who exemplifies this is the extremely popular Aberdeenshire poetess Flora Garry. The title poem of her collection *Benny-goak* is characteristic in its carefully accurate rendition of Buchan phonology (initial *f-* where other dialects have *wh-*: *fin, funn, fye*; medial *-dd-* for *-th-*: *fadder, midder, hedder*; the *ee* vowel in *deen, eese, tee*) and its use of local words (*sklyter, clocher, sotter*). The association with a definite area is emphasised by the use of place-names, a device which Garry employs frequently. At least in this poem, she avoids the danger of excessive nostalgia and sentimentality: an obvious trap for writers in this mode. It is poetry of and for the North-Eastern farming community, and it pays some attention to the poverty, hardship and narrowness of farm life. This gives it a degree of realism which entitles it to the attention of a wider readership: it is not a mere Kailyard revival. However, Garry clearly has no pretensions to national stature. When she ventures beyond the confines of Buchan, the results demonstrate her minor status. The poem *War*, for example, which begins 'Faar's Baabie Jeanie's loon?', includes four verses dealing with local characters, and concludes 'Speir at the warsslin tides, the desert san's, the caul' starlicht. They ken faar', is effective enough, but obviously not to be compared with, say, *A Mither's Lament* by Sydney Goodsir Smith.

> ROUGER Ya knee-crept, Jesus-crept, swatchin little fucker, ah'll cut the bliddy scrotum aff ye! Ah'll knacker an gut ye, ah'll eviscerate ye! Ya hure-spun, bastrified, conscrapulated young prick, ah'll do twenty year fur mincin ye. You hear me? Ah'll rip ye fae the gullet tae the groin, ah'll incinerate ye! Ah had her— right therr—ah had her, spreadeagled, waitin fur the knife—an you blew it. You blew the chance o pittin wan in her, an wan on Charlie. He's never had her, but ah wid have had her. Anither minute, ah wid have scored where he's never scored, an you shankered it, ya parish-eyed, perishin bastart. Well, whit she didnae get, you'll get. Come doon here, come doon ah'm tellin ye, ah'll pit a shot in your arse that'll feel like thunder. Come doon ah tell ye, or are ye gaun tae stey up?

> Roddy McMillan, *The Bevellers*

Whereas rural dialects are typically regarded with affection and associated with a way of life which is seen as having at least some attractive qualities, urban Scots belongs to a life-style which would generally be seen as much less desirable. Writers aiming at a *verismo* style, depicting the harsh and savage aspects of working-class life in the cities, often employ a 'dense' Scots based on this form of speech. Roddy McMillan's play *The Bevellers* is a notable instance. It is set in a glazing shop, and deals with the first, and in the event the only day of a young boy's apprenticeship to the trade. What starts as rough humour on the part of the older hands and innocent *faux pas* on the boy's leads to real antagonism and cruelty, and the uncompromising realism of presentation makes this a powerful and disturbing play. The language of the passage quoted is self-explanatory: it is, obviously, that of a hard-man in a fury. Phonetically it is extremely realistic, as it also is in its fluent use of obscenities. This character, indeed, is astonishingly imaginative in his threats and curses: besides the usual repertoire of orthodox swear-words, he produces nonce concoctions such as *bastrified* and *conscrapulated.* Other examples from elsewhere in the play are *conshiterified, diabastric,* and *blohoorable.* (This type of language could be described as the modern counterpart of Dunbar and Kennedy's *Flyting*; just as, to cite the opposite end of the spectrum of linguistic creativity, Sydney Goodsir Smith's use of Latin- or French-derived inventions such as *orsplendant, granderie, velvous, scelartrie,* is the modern counterpart of the Makars' aureate diction.)

> Doon nyir hungkirz. Wheesht.
>
> > nay fornirz ur communists
> > nay langwij
> > nay lip
> > nay laffn ina sunday
> > nay g.b.h. (septina wawr)
> > nay nooky huntn
> > nay tea-leavin
> > nay chanty rasslin
> > nay nooky huntn nix doar
> > nur kuvitn thir ox
>
> Oaky doaky. Stick way it
> —rahl burn thi lohta yiz.

Tom Leonard, *Feed ma Lamz*

If a colloquial register is used for subjects which would naturally be associated with a literary register, the result can be potently ironic. Tom Leonard in *Feed ma Lamz* takes the Ten Commandments (or nine of them: the one relating to idolatry appears to have been dropped from this version) and demonstrates what they might be imagined to have become in the atmosphere of ignorance and bigotry for which Glasgow is—justly or otherwise—notorious. His orthography is highly idiosyncratic. Often it is simply a phonetic representation of the sound of Glasgow speech (*doon nyir.., huntn* (the *t*, of course, representing a glottal stop), *way it*); but features like the *g* in *hungkirz*, the final *z* in this word and other plurals, the final *j* in *langwij*, the *aw* digraph in *wawr*, suggest no pronunciation different from that represented by the orthodox spelling. The effect of such mis-spellings is rather to convey the impression of illiteracy, and by implication stupidity, on the part of the supposed speaker: who is, of course, not the actual Deity of Judaism or Christianity, but the notion of God which some people—on the evidence of their behaviour—might hypothetically be presumed to have. The language is firmly rooted in the colloquial register, not only by its phonology, but also by the use of idioms such as *language* (i.e. bad language) and slang expressions such as *tea-leavin, chanty rasslin*, and *g.b.h.* (i.e. grievous bodily harm).

> Ah hate in love
> an how this comes aboot
> ye'll mebbe wahnt tae know.
> Well, ah don't know.
> Ah only know it happens,
>
> goad, ah know.

David Neilson, Ah hate in love

Another instance of the unexpected use of a colloquial register is the group of translations from Catullus by David Neilson. Whereas Leonard, by writing of a noble subject in undignified language, achieves a pungently satiric effect, Neilson's intention is rather to give realism and contemporary relevance to the Roman poet. By rendering his works in a realistic dialect, he is able to emphasise the disconcerting familiarity, despite the difference in time, language and culture, of Catullus' subject matter.

A sair stramash—a hairse wee quinie quavers
On hauflin love, her sang a wheen o havers;

A bourach o hardly-happit jigtime burdies
Gae yokan barebuff wames til a yark o hurdies;

Three babbity blondes, three pouter-doos, are cooan,
Their sheil a rickle o chords in rowters' ruin;

A gasterous fraik, his phizz as grim as gorgon
Maks lounderan love til a less-nor-michty organ;

A bonny bucko, gifted (by God?) til tumphies,
Stounds like a stirk, and back they grain like
                                      grumphies;

A spanky spade lats lowse as heich a yammer
As tines aa sense (langsyne he tint aa grammar);

And loud or laich, but deavan aye the lughole,
The gueetars gowp like watter doun the plughole;

O wash awa this weird! O sain this passion!
This pyne o youth that stangs wi sair stramashin!

Alexander Scott, *Big Beat*

At first sight, the dominant effect of this poem is an irony of
the opposite type from that of *Feed ma Lamz*: the use of a
literary register for a trivial subject. The language, however,
is not entirely literary but contains an admixture of colloquialisms; and the effect of the mixing of registers is
humorous and satirical. Familiar Scots words abound:
*stramash, wheen, hurdies, stirk, grumphies, rickle, bonny,
weird.* Most of them are still in active use in both speech and
writing, and some have literary associations (the rhyme
burdies – hurdies of course appears in *Tam o Shanter*). There
are also some rare and purely literary words: *gasterous, pyne,
sain.* Interspersed among those are words from the vocabulary of slang or pop jargon: *phizz, bucko, tumphies, lughole,
spanky, spade.* The language, in fact, is a peculiar mixture of
literary and colloquial. This feature is observable on levels
other than that of vocabulary. Similes, a literary feature, are
present; but they are extremely undignified examples (*like a
stirk, like grumphies, like watter doun the plughole*). Rhyme is
invariably used, but several of the rhymes are 'pointed' in a
way not normally associated with serious poetry (*cooan –*

ruin, quavers – havers, lughole – plughole). The unexpected combination of colloquial and literary features in this poem results in a highly entertaining piece of satire.

The mixing of registers, however, is a device which entails risks, and not all attempts have been as successful as this. Sydney Goodsir Smith's play *The Stick-Up* is an example. A predominantly naturalistic play set in the Glasgow slums during the Depression, it clearly should have been written in colloquial Scots. On the whole, the style is appropriate: accurate renditions of Glasgow idioms such as *Gies ye a richt grue, sae it does, He was feart the polis was on to him, It's tuim, isn't it no?, Been robbin a bank, like, sonnie?, Lea me be, ye bluidy clype ye* are present in abundance. However, the dialogue also contains purely literary words such as *dowie, puirtith, wanhope, mapamound, granderie,* archaic grammatical features such as *I likena,* and poetic turns of phrase such as *The men whase sauls ye steek your belly wi.* Features of this kind have an inescapably jarring effect in the context of a realistic drama.

The 'literary' end of the scale of Scots writing has a wide range of possible uses; those at the 'colloquial' end are somewhat more limited. However, as this paper has tried to show, the functions of colloquial Scots in literature are numerous and varied. Yet despite the vast expressive potential of the Scots language in all its registers, an enormous range of possibilities has *not* been exploited. Scots is used almost exclusively for literature. Whereas the use of Gaelic for textbooks, official documents and reports, forms, road-signs, and other non-literary purposes is either an actual achievement or a serious possibility, even the idea of using Scots in such contexts sounds far-fetched. Readers who are perfectly well accustomed to poetry or dialogue in Scots often experience a feeling of strangeness when faced with, say, an editorial, book review or announcement in the language, such as those published in the *Lallans* magazine. Literature in Scots, besides, is more often than not about Scotland. Of course, this is no more than a generalisation, and counter-examples abound. The poetic treatment by Tom Scott and Sydney Goodsir Smith of great mythological and classical subjects, and Alexander Scott's adventurous experimenting with topics ranging from the Vietnam war to Jayne Mansfield, immediately spring to mind. However, the observation is still 'more often than not' true of Scots poetry, and almost invariably true of Scots prose. Stories in Scots have—with no exception known to me—a Scottish setting and Scottish characters; and such few attempts at non-literary prose as have appeared in Scots are—again with no exception known to me—discussions of Scots writers, comments on the use of the Scots language, suggestions for Scots spelling reform, or similar Scottish topics.

Superficially, this seems merely natural; but this is simply because we have become accustomed to accepting without question a limited role for Scots. In reality, there is no fundamental reason why Scots should not be used for, say, a story with a Wild West setting, a historical account of Sino-Japanese relations, or a critical article on Baudelaire or Philip Larkin. Of course such writings would look strange at first, but only because they have no precedents. Once a number of experiments along such lines had been conducted and a tradition had been established, the practice of using Scots for non-Scottish topics would no longer seem remarkable. Gaelic, in this respect too, is in at least slightly better case. Iain Crichton Smith's short stories range widely in space and time, including among other things sketches on Biblical and historical characters. The magazine *Gairm* contains articles on a variety of topics: Girvan Mackay, for example, has recently produced a discussion of the Norwegian language revival and a summary grammar of Quechua (the indigenous language of Peru). The initial oddity of seeing a language used for an unaccustomed purpose has not yet been overcome even in the case of Gaelic: I have heard Iain Crichton Smith's story *An Solus Ur*, which deals with the American President suffering from a family crisis while about to fire the missiles, criticised adversely (by a Gaelic speaker) on the grounds that the President and his associates would not be speaking Gaelic. Though speciously reasonable, this is in fact irrelevant: no more would they be speaking French, yet presumably nobody would object on that ground to a similar story written in French. Crichton Smith and his colleagues are attempting to extend the range of uses of Gaelic to include things with which the language has not hitherto been associated, and such attempts are urgently necessary. A fully mature language is capable of being employed for all purposes.

In Scots, experiments such as these have hardly begun. Scots is already well-established as a vehicle for poetry, it is coming to be used for fiction, and tentative attempts are being made at employing it for non-literary writing. However, except in poetry—and even there, only to a limited extent—Scots has not yet ventured out of Scotland. In the development of the language, this is the next breakthrough that will have to be made.

1 Kingsley Amis, *Take a Girl like You* (London: Gollancz, 1960) p 9.
2 Lewis Grassic Gibbon, *Sunset Song* in *A Scots Quair* (London: Hutchinson, 1967) p 84.
3 Truman Capote, 'Jug of Silver' in *A Tree of Night and Other Stories* (Harmondsworth: Penguin, 1967) p 66.

PART TWO

ENGLISH IN SCOTLAND

Papers on the characteristics, history and situation of the Standard English speech of Scotland.

4

The Status of English in and furth of Scotland

Tom McArthur

In this paper I want to discuss World English and Scots English, and to do so I must indicate fairly explicitly what I intend by these terms.

I can begin with the easier definition: 'World English' means the whole English language in all its varieties, everywhere, and all its users, past and present, with all their books and records. One area within this mass is 'World Standard English', a more or less homogeneous range of internationally acceptable norms of spelling, grammar, vocabulary and pronunciation.

Using this as my starting point, I can then say that within World English there are the various distinctive—usually national—varieties, one of which we can call 'Scots English'. This is the term by which I shall refer to all the varieties of speech in Scotland that derive (ultimately) from Anglo-Saxon, including the localised forms known as 'broad Scots' and 'dialect Scots'. It will also include, necessarily, something that I shall call 'Scottish Standard English', a more or less homogeneous range of nationally acceptable norms of spelling, grammar, vocabulary and pronunciation, which is in turn one variety of World Standard English.[1]

There has always been a certain ambiguity in the use of national and regional labels for kinds of English. The term 'Irish English', for example, might mean all forms of English in Ireland, or simply the standard forms. Worse, the term 'American English' can mean all the forms of English or only the standard ones in either the United States or the whole of North America. And worse still, the term 'English English' is hardly ever used, least of all by the inhabitants of England, because they feel that it is either unnecessary or inelegant or perfectly well served by the other ambiguous term 'British English'.

If we adopt the device proposed above, then we can make useful distinctions and can talk, elegantly and accurately enough, about an English Standard English which is different from the standards in Scotland and Wales, and a British Standard English, which subsumes them all. More importantly for the purposes of this book, however, we can use three separate but related terms unambiguously to talk about the condition of English in Scotland: Scots English for the totality, Scots for the localised vernaculars, and Scottish Standard English for the national variety of World Standard English.

To facilitate an ongoing discussion of English in Scotland and in particular its standard forms here, I have divided this paper into two parts. The first part discusses language at large and language in society, dealing with our ideas of the separateness of languages and the relationship between a 'language' and its 'dialects'. In this part I hope to give some psychological reality to the terms 'World English' and 'Scots English'. In the second part, however, I shall enter into some specific matters concerning the place of Scots English in the world today, and make some suggestions for further exploration and future action. It seems to me that we live in an interesting and important time for Scots English.

Bipolarism in Language
A capacity for language is supposed to distinguish mankind from the rest of the animal kingdom. The possession of distinct languages certainly helps to divide off whole masses of mankind one from the other. There is a kind of cliché which says that a common language indicates a common culture among its speakers (wherever they may be), but when thinking about this we should recall the ironic comment that the Americans and the British are two peoples divided by the same language. The possession of the same language may make life easier for human beings when trying to communicate, but it does not *ipso facto* mean unity of thought or purpose or whatever. Since the time of Edward Sapir and Benjamin Lee Whorf it has been axiomatic that to some extent the language of a community shapes its view of the world, for example that Arabic goes with, and helps to shape, a subtly different world-view from, say, German. Today there are more than three hundred million people using the English language as their first or only language, and we are entitled to ask questions about the degree to which they all see the universe in the same way simply *because* they share the same language. This is a point to which I intend to return.

In his book *Elements of General Phonetics*,[2] Professor David Abercrombie talks about what he calls 'indexical features', and he says that these are different from 'linguistic features'. Linguistic features serve to identify a language and to demarcate it, to allow a comparison between that language and other languages. Indexical features, however, serve to show up differences among speakers of the *same* language. He gives a Biblical illustration of this. The Gileadites and Ephraimites were fighting at the river Jordan. The Gileadites won and sought to kill every Ephraimite who tried to escape across the river. There were, however, many Gileadites crossing too, and unfortunately both tribes looked disconcertingly like each other. The Gileadites, therefore, used an indexical feature in their common language, Hebrew, to solve the problem of identity. The guards asked each passing man to say the word *shibboleth*, and, of course, as everyone knew in those days, a true Ephraimite couldn't pronounce *sh*. He said *sibboleth* instead—and was promptly slaughtered. You could imagine a Scots horde entangled with an English horde at the River Tweed, people killing or sparing depending on whether the informant put an /r/ in *the law of England* or could say *Loch Lomond*. Indexical features are potent things; we may not kill each other at the present time on such flimsy pointers, but when we hear them all sorts of warning bells ring. Depending on one's education, politics, class, region, social psychology and personal hang-ups, these warning bells ring for good or for ill.

Most of us accept a political element in language, but this element is sometimes more subtly powerful than we care to reflect on. The names of languages, for example, are often political. If, for example, the Netherlands had been absorbed by Germany when that state was being formed, then 'Dutch' might have been regarded simply as a form of 'Deutsch', some kind of Low German. The Dutch, however, have no wish to associate themselves with the German language and, while accepting that their language is Germanic, they give it a separate title. It is, they insist, a 'language' and not a 'dialect'. If there had been a political union in Scandinavia instead of three states, then Swedish, Norwegian and Danish might have been seen as 'dialects' of a common Scandinavian. It would have been politically desirable to view them in that light. Instead, each nation proudly asserts its individuality, and has its own neat little spelling conventions to prove it. This suggests that if you do not have clear-cut indexical features to show that you are different, then you will soon *adopt* some. Again, certain nations tend to identify themselves strongly and emotionally with a language, as for example France and the French language. A moment's thought, however, reminds us—and the French—that the language exists vigorously in Belgium, Switzerland and several post-colonial states, and that in France itself minorities identify themselves with 'Basque' and 'Breton' first and French second. A state and a language are not necessarily coterminous.

Nevertheless, the terms 'language' and 'dialect' are clearly useful terms, as long as we do not become their slaves. In talking about them I would like to introduce a distinction which I have found helpful in teaching English to foreign learners, and in talking to teachers of English. On one side I would like to place what I call the 'little boxes' view of language and on the other the observable fact of language continuums. Many people (including, alas, eminent scholars down the years) have subscribed in varying degrees to the 'little boxes' point of view. There may be a little box called Latin and another called Spanish; the problem is, however, that in history we cannot point to the moment when Latin in Spain stopped and Spanish began. Similarly, people tend to label one box for a language (say, English) and inside they put lots of tidy smaller boxes, each labelled for a dialect. Well now, life is demonstrably a continuum and it is only a matter of procedural convenience to cut it up into manageable chunks. We can be deluded by our methods of classification and by the emotions that often go with them. Thus, with the tongues called English and Scots no-one can point to a stage in time or space where something English becomes something Scots—unless of course one were to point to Hadrian's Wall. In such a case, however, one would be making a political statement like the Dutch or the Scandinavians. It would have to be assessed as such, and the naming of languages would follow on the political decisions then taken. Undoubtedly a political decision will affect the continuum and tend to give more support to the illusion of little boxes neatly labelled, but the continuum does not therefore vanish although it may be to some extent broken. A journey along the Dutch–German border if not the Scottish–English border can clarify the mind on such points.

Additionally, there is nothing in history which suggests

that speakers of the same language from different areas *must* be intelligible to each other. If of course for administrative or educational reasons, or because you need a conscript army or whatever, you bring people into close contact and disseminate identical information to them all, then you may have to develop a little box for that purpose, modelling it on, say, the form of the language in use in the capital or in a university town or used for a religious book. This artefact is the new standard language, almost invariably of a nation-state, and its advocates have a commendable desire to 'fix' that language and to insist on correct or received usage. Social pressure towards such a convenient norm is very great and it takes on a new extended life of its own. In that way the idea of a little box is to some extent self-fulfilling, because the move towards a homogeneous speech community creates the very little box that you were talking about. But again, the continuum doesn't therefore vanish. There is in reality no little box, only an ideal of sorts, and a mass of approximations.

Now let us return to the question of World English, which is very much bound up with our idea of education and upward social mobility and the written word. Alf Garnett and Wullie McFlannel might just manage to discuss their problems in an army billet or a construction camp, but for practical purposes within the totality of World English there is something else which is now very noticeable: a World Standard English towards which writers, publishers, teachers, newspapers, governments and so on are all moving. This World Standard English is astonishingly uniform: the points where it meets are far more significant than the natural or artificial indexical features which mark off the various constituent speech communities. Such a standard is a matter of convergence, a coming-together of the various communities, while at the same time there are in each community forms of speech which are highly divergent. Such is the human preoccupation with differences (and perhaps the need for differences) that we usually spend more time debating indexical features such as differences in American and British spelling than in considering how *similar* American and British spelling are. We also get riled if our favourite usage is abused; whence all the Letters to the Editor about the other fellow's solecisms, or about the language going to the dogs and why don't people pay attention to the indexical features that characterise the Queen, or Fowler, or the BBC?

There would appear to be a World Standard English, spoken as well as written. When I speak it, I do so with special indexical features, which could of course be anything linguistic, in syntax or in semantics, in intonation or in the pronunciation of vowels and consonants. Mostly, when I speak publicly, my indexical features are restricted to sound, to accent. My vocabulary is international and by and large academic; otherwise some of my listeners might not be able to thole my observations and so take a scunner at what I've got to say. Others might be relieved to catch a few words that are not normally part of the international repertoire. A listener with a reasonable ear can tell quite a lot about me by listening to my accent, just as he can tell quite a lot about other speakers by listening to theirs. We listen of course on two levels: to the content of the message and to the indexical features of the medium, and we make adjustments to the message accordingly. We might never admit to this—to being conditioned by the *how* of someone's delivery—but we are, and such responses are often more important than our responses to *what* the person seeks to say.

The major point I want to make at this stage, apart from underlining the potency of accent, is that whatever World Standard English is, it is not an accent. It is certainly concerned with the norms of syntax and semantics and the alphabet and spelling (more or less), and it is probably also a matter of rhythm and also sometimes of intonation, but there is little evidence to suggest that it relates to accent. It may relate to some extent to some *modifications* in accent that people are prepared to make in cosmopolitan company, but not to accent as such. There is, of course, plenty of evidence that many people have *wanted* it to relate to accent (usually only one particular accent), and that certain accents have had a powerful impact in different places. We acquire our accents early in life, and they are to some extent elastic, and yet they can be remarkably resistant to change. This resistance is partly the way we learned in childhood to use our mouths, but partly also a question of social identification. If there is an impetus to change our accents, what are our opinions of the direction in which we are asked to go? Are we doing the choosing, or are we being pushed? Do we feel that we will gain more or lose more by giving up those indexical features that mark our community from all others?

The idea of changing our set of indexical features as a chameleon changes colour is another of these 'little boxes' situations. It assumes that we can somehow stop sounding Glaswegian, say, and start sounding something else. Again, however, there is a continuum. A Glaswegian moving to London may assimilate towards whatever speech community he finds himself in there; some will assimilate more than others. If he or she (like the pop-singer Lulu) feels it to be in their interests they will make a thorough job of it for certain purposes; otherwise (like Billy Connolly) they won't. It is partly unconscious and partly conscious, a sliding action from one pole to another pole.

I am indebted to Mr A J Aitken for this idea of a *bipolar* situation, to describe people's progress along continuums. I would like to take the term a wee bit further and talk of *bipolarism* as a natural human condition. It is not the only term in use, and I should like also to mention *diglossia*, the term used by the American linguist Charles Ferguson in 1959.[3] In his paper he says:

> In many speech communities two or more varieties of the same language are used by some speakers under different conditions. Perhaps the most familiar example is the standard language and regional dialect as used, say, in Italian or Persian, where many speakers speak their local dialect at home or among friends of the same dialect area but use the standard language in communicating with speakers of other dialects or on public occasions.

It seems to me that a Scots audience can find something nearer home than Italian and Persian, in the well-named 'classroom language' and 'playground language' of our own children. Ferguson highlights the hang-ups that can go with such diglossia (the very word suggests a kind of schizophrenic Jekyll-and-Hyde situation). There are problems of prestige and embarrassment and social mobility tied into it, and even self-deception, he argues. For example, he maintains that if a person asks an educated Arab to help him learn Arabic, the Arab will normally seek to teach him Classical Arabic, although direct observation shows that it is useless in everyday situations. However, he is acting in all good faith, and it is possible to break through his self-deception by asking what kind of language he uses when speaking to his mother, his children, or his servants. Ah, he says, well they

don't of course understand Classical Arabic, that's true. . . .
This is reminiscent of the practice (not yet dead, alas) of
teaching foreign learners English through Shakespeare.

The term *diglossia* is probably a bit too sharp: it suggests
a box for the standard and a box for the other kind of
language. Consider for instance the work of David DeCamp
on Jamaican English, described in a paper in 1971.[4] He
says that there is a social continuum on the island, from a
Jamaican Standard English at one end to the 'broad creole'
or 'broken language', so-called, at the other. He then says what
I think is also significant for Scots:

> Each Jamaican speaker commands a span of this
> continuum, the breadth of the span depending on the
> breadth of his social activities. . . . A housewife may
> make a limited adjustment downward on the con-
> tinuum in order to speak with a market woman, and
> the market woman may adjust upward when she talks
> to the housewife. Each of them may then believe that
> she is speaking the other's language, for the myth
> persists in Jamaica that there are only two varieties of
> language—standard English and 'the dialect'—but the
> fact is that the housewife's broadest dialect may be
> closer to the standard end of the spectrum than is the
> market woman's 'standard'.

That is a pretty good description of bipolarism. A lot of work
remains to be done on the subject, and particularly on Scots
bipolarism,[5] but once we have a few names for phenomena of
this kind we can at least begin to think systematically about
them. This book is designed in part to assist people in
thinking about such things. Some questions that I can begin to
debate here can be further elucidated over the next few
years. They include these two questions:

1   What is the web of relationships between the popular
    forms of English—the playground language and so on—in
    Scotland, and the forms at the other end of the con-
    tinuum, where they shade into World Standard English?

2   What is the relationship between Scottish Standard Eng-
    lish and the other national standards, and in particular how
    does it relate to its neighbour in southern England, one
    accent of which has often been identified as a 'British' norm
    and considered the 'best' or preferred form of spoken
    Standard English?

The Scots and their English

In this part I am going to look at the place of Scots English in the world, and to start off I would like to compare England with West Germany, and Scotland with Austria. First of all, we have a country, Germany, where the name for its citizens and the name for its language are the same: 'German'. This predisposes the citizens, naturally enough, to think of German as *their* language. However, next door is another country, Austria, with a different name, which has been using the same language for the same length of time. The educated speakers of both countries have no trouble understanding each other, but everybody knows that there is something different about Austrian German. Clearly, to be specific, it will sometimes be necessary to talk about 'German German' and 'Austrian German'. The first of these may seem tedious to the Germans, but not to the Austrians. This I would suggest parallels pretty closely the state of affairs in this island, except that we have an umbrella term 'British' which complicates matters. 'English English' and 'Scots English' would seem (and do seem to me) to be necessary terms, and the slight discomfort felt in England does not justify the frequent efforts (as we shall see shortly) to avoid the apparent clumsiness by talking about 'English English' as 'British English'. There *is* a British English, which can and should be contrasted with American English in questions of grammar and spelling, but it is a comprehensive term which includes all the Englishes of Britain. It cannot legitimately be pre-empted (and yet it often *is* pre-empted) for the specific speech patterns of southern England. Let me give you at this point the definition of British English offered in the American *Random House Dictionary*: 'The English language as spoken and written in Great Britain, especially in southern England.' This dictionary reflects usage of course, but in this matter usage can amount to falsification, as I hope to show. Suffice it to hope, at this point, that no Department of English or Linguistics or whatever in a Scots university would assist in the continuance of this malpractice.

'British English' then, if it is anything, is a shared commodity. Its Scottish element differs, however, in many ways from its English element. For example, the literature of England is, by and large, monolithic, centred on the development of the dialect of the South-East Midlands in the written form which has so much shaped standard written

English everywhere. In Scotland, however, literature is bipolar, with a literature which shares in the tradition of Shakespeare, Dryden, Keats and so on, and one which is indigenous (Scots 'vernacular' literature). There are of course works which have elements of both, as in Burns and Scott. Additionally, the English element of British English has no linguistic competitor, whereas Scots English shares the land and the loyalties of the people with another language, Gaelic, which has its own literature. At this stage we can compare Scotland with Wales or Belgium and say that it is a bilingual country.

With the two languages go two cultural poles, and so we are bipolar in another way. The fact that one of Scotland's languages is weak is irrelevant. As long as two people continue to speak Gaelic, Scotland will be a bilingual country. This view can be tabulated as follows:

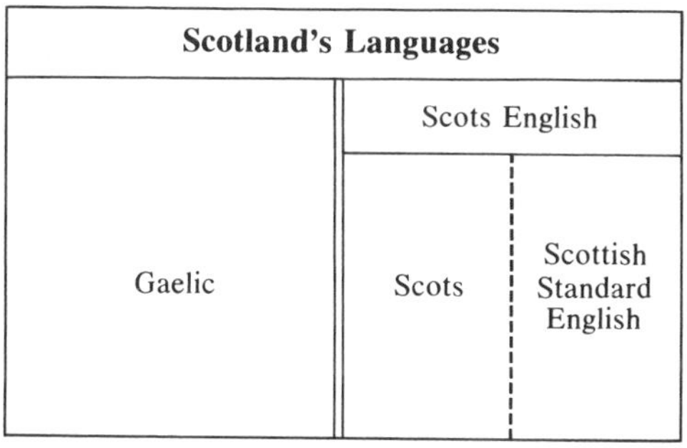

Scotland's Languages		
	Scots English	
Gaelic	Scots	Scottish Standard English

Figure 4:1

Let us be clear about the situation: Scotland is bilingual and bipolar between the English language and what it represents, and the Gaelic language and what it represents. Additionally, inside English, Scotland is bipolar between its national standard and its various forms of vernacular Scots. We know also that people swither a bit between these poles. Gaelic speakers carry elements of Gaelic into their English, and Gaelic radio programmes use many English loan-words in their Gaelic. We are aware that, consciously or unconsciously, a Scot can adjust the quality and style of his English in one direction or another, affecting pronunciation, grammar and vocabulary, and I commend this as a healthy activity. He has in fact an astonishing number of options and he can, if he feels the need, go down towards the English of England (as the comedian Ronnie Corbett does) or over towards the English of

America (as many of our singers do). The options are there, but with one proviso: he must use them well, because the penalty of doing it badly is the scorn of other Scots, if no one else.

There are certain long-standing problems associated in people's minds with shifting from one pole of English to another, and these are concerned with direction. Usually we shift one way and one way only, and social pressure has been largely in favour of our staying shifted once we have moved. No backsliding: the classroom language takes over and the playground language survives only in an occasional half-hearted joke or a moment of self-assertive nationalism of the 'Here's tae us, wha's like us' variety. I suggest that many folk would move more comfortably towards the pole of the world standard if they felt free to move back as often *and as far* as they wanted. You may have noticed that the Jamaican linguist talked about going 'up' and 'down' the continuum. Alas, too many people use this metaphor, because it is the metaphor of class and education, where 'dialect' is a nasty word. If we could substitute a different direction, such as 'across' or 'over' from one pole to the other, we would probably be describing the circumstances at least as well (if not better) and could slowly persuade people that long lapses into vernacular Scots are *not* the equivalent of secret sins which make you go blind.

It can be said with a lot of justification that for the last four hundred years, since the Bible was translated into an English literary form, Scots has been on the wane and that the standard is a standard of anglicisation meaning 'adapting towards England'. Of course, this is very true and not surprising in the light of the history of this elongated island. But we should also note that in the last hundred years a second influence has been at work on both the classroom and the playground languages, and that is the influence of the United States of America. Standards are the product not only of cliques who rule empires, but also of the endless interaction of travellers and writers and teachers and soldiers and sailors. We generally assume that it is a one-way traffic to our national detriment, but it may not be entirely so.

Let us look first of all at the view of Professor Randolph Quirk of University College, London. I am quoting from his *University Grammar of English*,[6] which is a distillation of his *Survey of English Usage*. In chapter 1 he describes Standard

English and the remarkable uniformity in the language throughout the world, but he names two national standards that are overwhelmingly predominant. He calls them American and British English, putting American first. There is no surprise in that if we use the definitions of British English which we examined a little earlier. However, a few paragraphs later he goes on: 'Scots, with ancient national and educational institutions, is perhaps nearest to the self-confident independence of British English and American English, though the differences in grammar and vocabulary are rather few.' Professor Quirk seems to have fallen into the pit which I mentioned earlier, but leaving that aside, let us consider what he intends by this. It would appear that he recognises a kind of English, mainly characterised by its accent, which is eligible for third place in the pecking order of international English. Well, that isn't bad, simply as a *per capita* assessment. He places Irish fourth, and perhaps the mass of the Scots and Irish would accept such an ordering. The important point is that, whatever the wording, this is an authoritative book and we come third in its league.

Let us look next at the introduction to the *Hamlyn Encyclopedic World Dictionary*, published in London in 1971. The editor, in a general discussion of standard and regional dialects, notes that the old South-East Midland dialect of England has become the dialect of 'the vast English middle class', and that when spoken with a Southern British English pronunciation it may even become the basis of international communication throughout the world. In the meantime, he says, other native dialects have been 'battered into submission' by education and the media. With *one* exception. He adds: 'In this connection a word should be said about the status of the speech of Edinburgh. Unlike any other standard of English, it has a history as long, intricate and fascinating as that of London. And unlike any other British dialect except that of London, it has won acceptance as the language of educated speakers outside the geographical area of its origin.'

These statements are straws in the wind. They belong to the Seventies. They indicate that Scottish Standard English has begun to be explicitly recognised and accorded a status which we have always suspected it should have.

There is more to it than that, however. In these explicit statements we have the tip of an iceberg of implicit acceptance which stretches back a century and more. To support this contention, I will stay in the world of dictionaries, which is a professional interest of mine. If we look into the major dictionaries of the English-speaking world (and there are a lot of them) we soon find that Scots forms are well-covered. If it is an American dictionary, specific British usage is marked and specific Scots usage is marked. If it is a dictionary produced in this island, then it has (I am happy to say increasingly) the American usages actually included and clearly marked, and Scots usage clearly marked. There are two reasons for this:

1   There are too many books in worldwide circulation written by Scots who have used a standard containing vocabulary and usages which are indexically Scottish. No self-respecting dictionary can ignore occurrences in Burns, Scott, Stevenson, Buchan and so on.

2   The world of dictionary-making is saturated with Scots, who seem to have a peculiar enthusiasm for it.

At this stage of the discussion we can turn to accent in Sam Johnson's time. In the late eighteenth century people were possessed by an enthusiasm for the correct pronunciation of English, and three 'experts' stand out: Walker the Englishman, Sheridan the Irishman, and Perry the Scotsman. Now let us listen to the allegation (to put it no stronger than that) of one John Pickering,[7] an observer of *American* English. In 1828 he wrote: 'It is often asserted, that the uniform pronunciation throughout New England is the true English pronunciation, handed down from past ages. But this we much doubt. We believe it has been brought about, if not entirely, yet principally, by means of the Scotch dictionary of Perry.' He goes on to quote a founder of the American dictionary tradition, Joseph Worcester, as justly observing that Perry's dictionary 'has been of great influence in fixing the prevailing pronunciation, especially in the Northern States.' He then adds that 'where we differ from the English, particularly in some of the vowels, it will be found that we agree with the Scotch.' There may be some doubt over the impact of dictionaries on people, but the United States has always been peculiarly susceptible to wordbooks, and it is significant that such men *believed* this Scots influence to have been there. There were of course large numbers of Scots settlers and we have the observation in 1928 of Professor Hans Kurath, the American dialectologist, that 'the North-and-West has at any events a Northern English (including Lowland Scotch) basis in stock and speech.'[8] One imagines that such a population bias would tend to favour a dictionary which encouraged their own practices.

That was the beginning. In 1850, an Aberdeen maths master, John Ogilvie, compiled the *Imperial Dictionary* (published by Blackie), based on the earlier American works of Noah Webster. This was an encyclopedic dictionary of the kind that Scots and Americans have always favoured and it had a famous revision in 1885 by another Scot, Charles Annandale. This version was reprinted in the States by the Century Company and became a main element in the development of one of the main streams of American lexicography, leading to the present-day Random House dictionaries. Ogilvie and Annandale were seminal in the States but had little influence in England. Credit for Ogilvie, however, was taken by the commentator J R Hulbert[9] who observed in 1955 that 'an Englishman, John Ogilvie, published the *Imperial Dictionary*.' Hulbert was himself an Englishman.

We can turn next to the great dictionary of the English language, begun by the Philological Society in 1858 and finished seventy years later. It was called the *New English Dictionary*. It owes its existence most of all to the work of a Scot, Murray, who himself edited half of the entire work. Of the other three copy-producing editors, one, Craigie, was a Scot and the two others were Englishmen. This work with its twelve volumes and supplements is a monument to Anglo-Scottish cooperation on their common language. The material was, however, housed latterly in Oxford and published by the Oxford University Press. Its name seems now to have become unshakably established as the *Oxford* English Dictionary. Because of the association of Oxford with a particular kind of English, this name is to be regretted. It reduces the compass of this tremendous work and also incidentally overshadows the place of the Philological Society in its creation.

Next, on this question of the Scottish hand in the making of dictionaries for the whole English-speaking world, we have the traditions of the Chambers brothers in Edinburgh and the Collins family in Glasgow. Chambers in particular have retained a distinctive Scottish cast to their products, especially in the *Twentieth Century Dictionary*, whose origins date back to at least 1867 if not to the 1830s. Like many makers of wordbooks, however, Chambers tend to be anonymous about the efforts of the individuals who make their books. Their names deserve to be better known, so that Donald and Patrick and Davidson and Geddie and Macdonald along with Ogilvie and Annandale and Murray and Craigie can all have their proper place in the roll-call of World English.

It is also not widely known that Peter Mark Roget of *Roget's Thesaurus* was trained as a doctor in Edinburgh and wrote for the *Encyclopaedia Britannica* which was at that time still based in Scotland.

Because of Scots settlers and dictionary-makers, the United States has tended to be more accommodating towards Scots English on the international stage than have many scholars in England. This is not to suggest that scholars in England have forgotten the existence of Scottish Standard English, but rather that they have tended and still tend to see it as out there, somewhere on the edge of things. Consider, for example, the opinion voiced in the earlier part of this century by an American with the significant name Fred Newton Scott. He said:

> ... one may recall that Scotland, Ireland and Wales are essential parts of the United Kingdom and as such are entitled to a voice, both literally and figuratively, in deciding questions of the King's English. To draw the suggested parallel, does not our Southern Speech (or Northern Speech, if the South prefers) have its counterpart in the pleasing and unmistakable accent of Scotchmen or Irishmen, and is not one just as good English as the other?[10]

Compare this generous and rational view made so many decades ago with one published recently in London and Oxford (1974). I am referring to the third edition of Hornby's dictionary for foreign learners of English, once called simply *The Advanced Learner's Dictionary of Current English* but in this edition the *Oxford Advanced Learner's Dictionary of Current English*. In the introduction, dealing with the pronunciation guide which is offered to foreigners, it says:

> In most cases the pronunciation shown is equally suitable for use with speakers from any part of the English-speaking world but, where this is not so, a choice of two forms is given, one representing the best known variety of British English, and the other the best known variety of American English.... One of them is known as General American; the other may be

conveniently termed General British . . . . In its own country each of them is the variety most associated with national broadcasting and least restricted in its geographical distribution.

This statement is reminiscent of the claim in the Hamlyn dictionary that the 'Southern British English accent' (better known as Received Pronunciation) will possibly become the accent of international communication. I do not wish to enter here into the question of what kind of accent or accents foreign learners of English need to seek, but I *am* concerned here with assumptions made by the Oxford editors. They talk of the 'best known variety of British English', and one may ask: best known to whom? They call the public-school accent of south-east England 'General British' because it is least restricted in geographical terms. Whose geography? And if we are discussing the representativeness of *any* accent and its 'Britishness', then is it not important to think also about class distributions and attitude distributions as well as geographical distributions?

One cannot escape a certain defensiveness when dealing with Scotland and England and the English language. Americans have felt the same sense of insecurity in the face of the perennial resounding confident claim from southern England to a monopoly on the norms of the international language. I have hoped to indicate here, however, that the world is changing and in a direction which favours the recognition of diversity in World Standard English. Like the Americans, the Scots have nothing to worry about, and a lot to gain by a bit of steady insistence.

Let me take one last example, a fine book by C L Barber of Cambridge and Leeds Universities. It is called *The Story of Language*.[11] Anyone reading this book can learn a great deal about language and can admire the liberalism of the writer. But I want to ask here a few questions about the implicit world view that underpins this book. You will recall that I started out by talking about whether all the folk of World English share the same view of things. You will note that Dr Barber entitles his book *the* story of language—not one story among many. He develops this story as a pyramid. At the start, with the broad base of the pyramid, he surveys all human language. He then chooses from among the languages the Indo-European family for particular study. From among the Indo-European languages he chooses English for special discussion, and in this unrolling evolutionary picture the spoken English of the southern public schools is given as representative of the latest development of English. It sits at the apex of the pyramid. The book was first published in 1964 and was revised in 1972. Now I could be accused of seeing something which is not there, or which wasn't intended. I am quite convinced that the writer meant no harm to anyone. You can rightly argue that the book was written for users of English, and that the Semitic language family and modern Israeli Hebrew would not interest them so much: all that is true. But I cannot help noting, after all these considerations, that the first use of 'British' comes on page 228 (in the thirteenth chapter) of a book 275 pages long, at a stage when the writer needs an adjective to indicate that English was spread throughout the world by the Scots, the Irish and the Welsh as well as the English.

I am not castigating Dr Barber, any more than an Indian would castigate a British historian for calling the events of 1857 the Indian Mutiny. It is all in your point of view, and my point is that a Scot or an American could not *by their background* have contrived the Story of Language in this way. Their angle of vision is different.

And here is the crux of the matter. We are one national variety of a vast international community of language users. This is in itself an exciting thought. We need books for tomorrow which take this adequately into account, and we all of us—Scots, English, Americans and so on—need research and attitudes of mind which allow for a healthier and more cosmopolitan view of English. I would suggest that the time is not far away when scholars and interested people from all over the English-speaking world will come together to talk about its unities and its diversities, its standards, its variants and its bipolarisms. And I can think of no better place for such a conference than this country, the third community in the pecking order of World English. I would personally be glad to see that conference come fairly soon.

1 For a model of Scots English see Table 6:1 (p 86), and for a sketch of the genealogical relation between vernacular Scots (the Scots Regional Dialects) and Modern Standard English see Figure 6:1 (p 87).

2 David Abercrombie, *Elements of General Phonetics* (Edinburgh University Press, 1967).

3 Charles A Ferguson, 'Diglossia' *Word* **15**, 1959, pp 325–340, reprinted in Dell Hymes (ed), *Language in Culture and Society* (New York: Harper & Row, 1964).

4 David DeCamp, 'Introduction: the study of pidgin and creole languages' in Dell Hymes (ed), *Pidginization and Creolization of Languages* (Cambridge University Press, 1971).

5 For some further discussion, see the first section of Chapter 6, and for some further references, see note 1 of that chapter.

6 Randolph Quirk & Sidney Greenbaum, *A University Grammar of English* (London:Longman, 1973).

7 John Pickering (1828), quoted in A W Read, 'The social impact of dictionaries in the United States' in Raven I McDavid Jr & Audrey R Duckert (eds), *Lexicography in English*. Annals of the New York Academy of Sciences, vol 211 (1973).

8 Hans Kurath, 'The origin of the dialectal differences in spoken American English' *Modern Philology* **25**, 1928, pp 385–395, reprinted in Juanita V Williamson & Virginia M Burke (eds), *A Various Language: Perspectives in American Dialects* (*New York*: Holt Rinehart & Winston, 1971).

9 James R Hulbert, *Dictionaries British and American* (London: André Deutsch, 1955, revised ed 1968).

10 Fred Newton Scott, 'The standard of American speech' *The English Journal* **6**, 1917, pp 1–15, reprinted in Williamson & Burke (see note 8).

11 C L Barber, *The Story of Language* (London: Pan Books, 1964, revised ed 1972).

5
The Accents of Standard English in Scotland

David Abercrombie

Although the conference from which the present section of this book derives was called *English As We Speak It In Scotland*, I am afraid that I cannot include myself in that 'we'. What I have to say is not based on analysis of my own speech, which originates in England, but on observations of the students in phonetics I have had in Edinburgh over the past twenty-eight years; or perhaps I should say it is based on what I have been able to learn from my students' (supervised) *self*-observation. I shall try to describe what I have learned with as little use of technicalities as I can.

I want to look at what it is that characterises the way Standard English is pronounced in Scotland, as compared with the rest of the English-speaking world; I want also to look at what variation in pronunciation exists within Scottish Standard English itself. I shall confine myself to the speech of the Lowlands, mainly because I do not know enough about Highland accents to say much that is useful about them. And I shall not, of course, be concerned with Scots properly so-called, as distinct from Standard English.

All accents, of all languages, have characteristic features of *intonation*, of *rhythm*, and of *voice quality*. These features are the least investigated aspects of Scottish Standard English, and there is not very much of importance, in the present state of our knowledge, to be said about them. I shall leave these features to the end. It is the so-called *segmental* features that I shall spend most time on: that is, the vowels and consonants of Scottish Standard English.

There are four respects in which the segmental features of related accents of a language can differ from each other. I shall list them first, and then go on to discuss each in turn. We can have, between accents,

   (i) *structural* differences,
   (ii) *systemic* differences,
   (iii) *distributional* differences, and
   (iv) differences of *phonetic realisation*.

(i) *Structural differences* between accents concern the freedom which specific phonemes have to combine with other phonemes to form *structures*, such as syllables or words, and more especially the various *restrictions, limitations*, or *constraints* which may exist on their freedom to combine or to occur in various places in structures.

Standard English in general, like most languages, has many restrictions on the freedom of segments to combine with each other. There is on sale in this country a brand of continental quilt called a *Fnug*. This as a trade name is curious, because it contravenes one of the structural restrictions of English, to the effect that a word cannot start with /fn/. (The restriction can be stated in more general terms.) Trade names, new slang words and other coinages, and words borrowed from other languages, are usually made to conform strictly with the English structural constraints; in fact combinations of sounds that do not comply are normally found difficult to pronounce by native speakers, and one wonders if *Fnug* will prove a successful name for this kind of quilt. Scots shares most of the structural constraints of the English-speaking world.

However, there is one structural aspect of English which is very important for our present purposes. All the accents of Standard English in the world fall into two classes, depending on whether they are subject to a certain structural restriction or not. This is a restriction on the occurrence of the phoneme /r/ (irrespective of how it may be pronounced; it has of course a wide variety of phonetic realisations in the English-speaking world), namely that /r/ can occur only before a vowel, and not before a consonant or before a pause. Some accents of Standard English are subject to this restriction and some are not. In the accents which are not subject to it, an /r/ can occur just as well before a consonant or a pause as before a vowel; it is a consonant just like any other consonant. These latter accents may be called *rhotic*, to use a convenient technical term which we owe to Dr J C Wells of University College, London. The other accents, then, are *non-rhotic*.

My own speech is non-rhotic. All Scottish Standard English accents, on the other hand, are rhotic. Accents of England are divided, very roughly, into those of the west, which are rhotic, and those of the east, which are non-rhotic (though rhotic *dialects*, as distinct from accents of Standard

English, can be found in the north-east, around Durham, and in the south-east, in Kent). Irish accents are rhotic. The whole of the middle-west and west of the USA is rhotic, though the east and the south are mostly non-rhotic. Most Canadian accents are rhotic; Australian and South African accents are non-rhotic. It is probably true to say that the majority of Standard English speakers in Britain are non-rhotic; and that the majority of Standard English speakers in the English-speaking world are rhotic. From this structural aspect, therefore, Scottish Standard English is a little unusual in Britain, but usual in the English-speaking world as a whole.

(ii) *Systemic differences* concern the number of different vowels and consonants that accents make use of for distinguishing meanings. We need to consider separately the system of consonants and the system of vowels. It is often convenient, too, when comparing accents, to consider sub-systems of various kinds. For instance it might be enlightening in some cases to separate a sub-system of word-initial consonants from a sub-system of word-final consonants, or a sub-system of vowels in stressed syllables from a sub-system of vowels in unstressed syllables; and so on.

It is systemic differences to which I wish to devote most of my time. They are not very conspicuous differences to the casual listener, but they are the most interesting differences linguistically.

(iii) *Distribution differences* have nothing to do with structural or systemic differences. They are more conspicuous; they are also linguistically more superficial. They are called distribution differences because they concern the way phonemes are *distributed* in words. Thus it is possible for there to be two accents which have the same consonant and vowel systems, and which have no structural differences, but which nevertheless have different phonemes in the same words. For example, two accents might have different vowel phonemes in *pat* and in *past*, but one might have *photograph* with the *pat* vowel in the last syllable, while the other has the *past* vowel in the last syllable. This therefore is a distribution difference between the two accents. People notice such differences very readily. There are many distribution differences between Scottish Standard English and most other accents of Standard English, both in vowels and in consonants. We find, for example, *housing, houses* with inter-vocalic /s/ rather than /z/; *December* with /z/ rather than

/s/; *sandwich* with medial /ŋ/ rather than /n/; and so on.
(iv) *Differences of phonetic realisation* are also independent
of structural or systemic differences. Two people speaking
the same language may sound very different from each other
and yet have identical consonant and vowel systems and no
structural differences. They sound different from each other
because they have different phonetic realisations for some or
all of the items in the systems. Differences of this sort, also,
are conspicuous, and although they may not be very important linguistically, they are often of great importance
socially—particularly in England, but also in other English-
speaking countries. Mr Heath, Sir Harold Wilson and Mrs
Thatcher, for example, have three noticeably different accents; but they differ almost entirely in this matter of the
phonetic quality of many of the phonemes in their vowel and
consonant systems. Scottish Standard English is in general
characterised by a number of differences of phonetic quality
from accents of England—from, indeed, accents of the greater
part of the English-speaking world. For example, many Scottish speakers have a realisation of /l/ which is not homorganic
with /t/, /d/, /n/, but is dental rather than alveolar. Very
noticeable dental allophones of /t/, /d/, and perhaps /n/, occur
when preceded by /l/, as in *world* compared with *word*, *belt*
compared with *bet*.

Let us now go back to *systemic differences*, and first of all to
the consonant system.

Consonant systems are really quite surprisingly uniform
in accents all over the English-speaking world. In fact it is
possible to speak of a 'general English consonant system'
which is the same, with the occasional omission or addition of
an item, for all Standard English speakers. Scottish Standard
English, which otherwise has the general English consonant
system, has one of these additions. This is the voiceless velar
fricative, /x/. No other accent of Standard English possesses
it. It is not a very common consonant, but nevertheless one
hears it frequently enough. It is found in proper names like
Buchan, Strachan; in loan-words from Gaelic, like *loch*; and,
from many speakers, in words like *technical, technique*. The
rest of the English-speaking world uses /k/ in all these words.

There is a great deal more to be said, from the systemic
point of view, about vowels than about consonants. Vowel
systems are certainly not uniform over the English-speaking

world and it is hardly possible to speak of a 'general English vowel system'. It is in this area that some of the most interesting things about Scottish Standard English are found. In England accents of Standard English do not vary a great deal from each other in their vowel systems but in Scotland there is considerable systemic variation. I would like at this point to refer to Table 5:1.

	Scotland	England
bead	*1* i	*1* i
bid	*2* ɩ	*2* ɩ
bay	*3* e	*3* eɩ
bed	*4* ε	*4* ε
(never	*4a* ë)	
bad	*5* a	*5* a
balm		*6* ɑ
not	*8* ɔ	*7* ɒ
nought		*8* ɔ
no	*9* o	*9* oɷ
pull	*11* u	*10* ɷ
pool		*11* u
bud	*12* ʌ	*12* ʌ
side	*13* ʌi	*14* aɩ
sighed	*14* ae	
now	*15* ʌu	*15* aɷ
boy	*16* ɔe	*16* ɒɩ

Table 5:1

I will explain in a moment what is implied by the headings 'Scotland' and 'England' and why I want to include England, but first I would like to say a word about how to interpret what is laid out in the Table. In the left-hand column there is a series of key-words, separated by ruled lines. These lines may be prolonged into the next column, like the line between *bead* and *bid*, or they may not, like the line between *bad* and *balm*. The absence of a line means the absence of a' distinction between the vowels of the adjacent key-words in the accent that the column represents; if a line is present, however, then there is a distinction, and therefore two separate phonemes are involved, not just one. Thus in the Scotland column it is clear that *bad* and *balm* contain the same vowel phoneme; in the England column the ruled line starts again, indicating that in that accent different vowel phonemes are used. In this way the contrasts between the two systems can be seen at a glance. The number of boxes in a column is the number of different items or phonemes in that system.

In Table 5:1 the phonemes are identified both by numbers and by symbols. The symbols are not of any great importance; they are convenient—they are used by our Scottish students when transcribing their own speech—but it would be possible to work out other systems of transcription just as good. The numbers provide a very convenient way of talking about the phonemes. They are not, of course, numbers for vowel *qualities* (as for example Cardinal Vowel numbers are), they merely identify the boxes and not their contents.

Let us now compare the two systems which are set out here. I have chosen one accent as representative of Scotland and another one as representative of England—one for Scottish Standard English and one for 'Anglo-English' (a convenient term for English Standard English recently introduced in the correspondence columns of *The Scotsman*). The Anglo-English system is the system of that famous accent called RP which, as everyone knows, stands for 'Received Pronunciation', but it is also the system of a number of other, non-RP, accents to be found in both the south and the north of England, and from both rhotic and non-rhotic speakers. It is the most general and the most commonly-used vowel system for Standard English in England, although there are, as a matter of fact, a few systemic differences to be found between accents there.

The Scottish system is also a common one, perhaps the commonest among Standard English speakers in Scotland (though I have not been able to verify this), but nevertheless it is only one of a number of Scottish Standard English vowel systems, all of them fairly common. I have named this system the 'Basic Scottish Vowel System'. (I ought to say, to prevent misunderstandings, that the 'immediate constituents' of that phrase are 'Basic' and 'Scottish Vowel System'; they are *not* 'Basic Scottish' and 'Vowel System'. Some people have taken them to be the latter, but what is meant is 'the basic vowel system of Scottish Standard English' and not 'the vowel system of Basic Scots'. It is necessary to say this, because although there is no such thing as Basic Scots (which seems a nonsensical expression to me), I nevertheless often hear people using the term—having got it, I am afraid, through misinterpreting that phrase of mine.)

I have called it the Basic Vowel System because the other Scottish Standard English vowel systems are best described in terms of departures from it: it provides a *basis* for the description of the other systems. In other words it is *descriptively* basic. I do not know if it could be said to be basic in any other sense, although I think one could perhaps say fairly enough that it is the most *Scottish* of the vowel systems of Standard English in Scotland. It seems to me that more than half of our students use it (though many who come from Edinburgh do not).

Let us begin by considering the vowel which is numbered *4a*. I have put it in brackets because it is a kind of 'floating' vowel—it is not an integral part of any Scottish vowel system. It can in fact occur with any of them, which is rather an odd situation. That is why I have numbered it *4a*, so that it can be inserted into any system without upsetting the numbering of the items following it. Examples of words in which it is found, in addition to *never*, are *ever, every, seven, seventy, eleven, heaven, devil* (I think all those *v*s are probably co-incidence), *twenty, next, shepherd, whether, bury,* and others.

This vowel might perhaps fairly be called 'Aitken's Vowel', because as far as I know no-one had noticed it until Mr A J Aitken drew my attention to it in, I think, 1949. Before that it seems never to have been mentioned in any discussion of Scottish Standard English. Its phonetic quality may be the reason why it escaped notice for so long. It is a fairly centralised vowel, not a fully front one; in fact it sounds very like the vowel *I* use when *I* say *never*—my number *4* vowel is always rather centralised and sounds markedly different from the fully front, or 'peripheral', vowel used by Scots in, for example, the word *dead*. This phonetic similarity between the Anglo-English *4* and the Scottish Standard English *4a* may explain the failure in the past to identify the latter as a separate systemic item.

There are a few minor points to be noted about this vowel. Firstly, it has no equivalent in any Anglo-English system, or indeed in any vowel system of the rest of the English-speaking world, as far as I know. Secondly, it is not to be considered as forming part of the Basic System. It is inserted in the Table for convenience, but in brackets to show its special status. Thirdly, it seems to have a regional basis; it is found in the West of Scotland, in the Borders, and in Perthshire, for example. I formerly believed it was not to be found in Edinburgh, but Mr Aitken has shown me that I was wrong in this. Its geographical distribution needs further investigation. Fourthly, speakers who have vowel *4a* in their system show great distribution differences between each other; moreover some speakers use it in only a very few words (which means it can very easily escape detection in those speakers, and an investigator may not notice it even after spending quite a lot of time on such an informant), while others use it in quite a lot of words. Lastly, it appears to occur only in stressed syllables.

The Basic Vowel System is not the only Scottish Standard English system. The other systems are best described as modifications of the Basic System towards the Anglo-English system, which is why the right-hand column of Table 5:1 is there. These are not random modifications; as we shall see, they form a hierarchy. Although they are almost certainly due to influence from England, they are not modifications made by *individuals* to their own speech in imitation of Anglo-English speakers. These other systems are genuine Scottish systems, properly institutionalised, transmitted from parents to children or learnt by children from contemporaries at school. The actual influence from England may have taken place quite far back in time, perhaps in the eighteenth century. A Scot using a vowel system containing some of these modifications towards the Anglo-English system might never even have met an Englishman. We have therefore a *series* of Scottish Standard English vowel systems, and we shall see that they are related to each other in a rather interesting way.

The first modification to the Basic System introduces a distinction corresponding to the Anglo-English distinction between *5* and *6* (you will notice that the Scottish vowels are so numbered in the Table that you can insert these additions without upsetting the numbering). Quite a lot of people, particularly in Edinburgh, have this augmented system containing a *5/6* distinction, but curiously enough we find distribution differences between this Scottish system and the normal Anglo-English system, where the former has *6* but the latter *5*. This, I believe, is one of the signs of the antiquity of this Scottish system: one would not expect these distribution differences if the influence from England were more immediate. For example, Anglo-English speakers say *gather*, *salmon* with number *5*, whereas Scottish speakers with a *5/6* distinction usually say these words with number *6*. The following are some of the other words I have noticed which may have *6* in Scottish English but *5* in Anglo-English: *value*, *alphabet, parallel, paragraph* (in the first syllable), *Cramond*.

Next, a distinction may be added to the Basic System corresponding to the Anglo-English distinction between *7* and *8*—between *not* and *nought*, that is to say. Here again one finds distribution differences between those Scots who have this distinction and speakers in England. The following words, for example, may be pronounced with number *8* in Scotland but number *7* in England: *lorry, squash, squad, watch, wash, yacht*. The interesting thing about the modification of the Basic System by the introduction of this *7/8* distinction is that it is always accompanied by the presence of the *5/6* distinction. Not everybody who distinguishes *5* and *6* also distinguishes *7* and *8*, but the converse *is* the case: everybody who distinguishes *7* and *8* also distinguishes *5* and *6*. The presence of the former distinction implies the presence of the latter. I have not so far found an exception to this.

A third modification to the Basic System is possible and it is easy to guess what this is: the introduction of a distinction between *10* and *11*. This is rather rare and is inconsistently maintained by some of the speakers who have it. It is always accompanied by a *5/6* distinction and a *7/8* distinction, I have found. Distribution differences from Anglo-English speakers may be found here too, e.g. the word *food* may be pronounced with *10* in Scotland but it usually has *11* in England.

So we have four different Scottish vowel systems: the Basic System; the Basic plus a *5/6* distinction; the Basic plus a *5/6* and also a *7/8* distinction; and the Basic plus these two distinctions and also a *10/11* distinction. These are all modifications away from the Basic System towards the England system but, curiously, they do not make the accents which have these augmented systems *sound* any more English than those that do not. In fact, oddly enough, they tend to have the opposite effect, and make them sound more Scottish, because of the very conspicuous distribution differences that I mentioned—they are much more noticeable to the ordinary listener's ear than systemic differences. Thus someone who says *salmon* or *gather* with the (originally Anglo-

English) number 6 vowel sounds strikingly Scottish simply because 6 is not used in those words in England.

There are two other means by which the Basic System can be augmented. Firstly, any of the four systems can have vowel number 4a added, producing, in effect, a further four systems. This, of course, is not a modification towards Anglo-English. Secondly, there is one more way in which any of the vowel systems enumerated so far can be modified, and which also is not a modification towards Anglo-English; this concerns vowel *length* or *quantity*.

As far as I know, in all accents of Scottish Standard English, vowels are long in final stressed open syllables, such as in *agree*, or *brew*, as indeed they are in all accents of Standard English. Scots is exceptional, however, in that if an inflection such as *-d* of the past tense is added to these words, the final vowel maintains its length, whereas in nearly all other accents of English it is shortened. This means that for most Scots speakers there is a distinction of vowel length between *greed*, with a short vowel, and *agreed*, with a long vowel; and similarly between *brood* (short) and *brewed* (long). In most other accents of English the vowels would be the same length. This, of course, is a well-known fact.[1] It would be misleading to take these differences of vowel length as part of the vowel system. It is not so well known, however, that some Scottish accents carry contrasts of vowel length further; they make them where there is no question of an inflection being added. A fairly widespread example of this is a difference between the two words *creek*, with a short vowel, and *creak*, with a long vowel (the vowel quality being the same in both cases). Other examples which I have found of the same kind of opposition of vowel quality are:

short vowel	long vowel
leek	leak
choke	joke
made	maid
badge	cadge

The etymological reasons for these differences are not obvious. Other accents of Standard English occasionally make such differences. Some Australian accents, for instance, distinguish *badge* and *cadge* by a vowel length difference, although oddly enough it is *cadge* that has the short vowel in this case, and *badge* the long one (see D Laycock, *Le Maître*

Phonétique, 1966, p 22). In Northern Ireland, in County Antrim, *spoke* (of a wheel), with a short vowel, is distinguished from *spoke* (from *speak*) with a long one. (See R J Gregg, *Orbis,* 7, 1958, pp 392–406. Gregg thinks this opposition between long and short may be an innovation; it is more likely to be an importation from Scotland.)

These length differences distinguish (monomorphemic) words, and are therefore systemic. Here, therefore, is another possible modification to the Basic Vowel System, one which can be combined with any of the other modifications. Thus we have a whole hierarchy of Scottish vowel systems, which can be summarised as follows.

Basic System	13 items		
BS + 5/6	14 items	+ 4a	+ quantitative
BS + 5/6, 7/8	15 items		opposition of vowels
BS + 5/6, 7/8, 10/11	16 items		

Figure 5:1

Table 5:1 sets out, in the Scotland column, the complete Basic Vowel System; the other augmented systems discussed so far can also be fitted into it. What appears in the England column, however, is not a complete vowel system, and no complete Anglo-English system can be fitted into it. All the vowel systems of Anglo-English contain additional items that do not appear there. This can be made clear by means of two further tables setting out two sub-systems of vowels, in the same manner as in Table 5:1.

The first of these, Table 5:2, gives those items of the Basic Scottish vowel system which appear in syllables closed by /r/, together with the Anglo-English equivalents of these vowels—although of course, Anglo-English being non-rhotic, no /r/ follows them. (Vowel *4a* is placed within brackets here, as it is in Table 5:1. Those Scots speakers who have the vowel in their system are as likely to use it before /r/ as in any other context. Those who do not have it replace it here, as elsewhere, by *4.*)

Notice that several members of the Anglo-English vowel system—mostly diphthongs—appearing in Table 5:2 were not encountered previously in Table 5:1, i.e. *17, 18, 19, 20* and *21.* (Many speakers of Anglo-English replace *20* by *8.*)

	Scotland	England
first	*2* ɩ	
word	*12* ʌ	*17* ɜ
heard	*4* ɛ	
(herd	*4a* ɛ̈)	
here	*1* i	*18* ɩə
fair	*3* e	*19* ɛə
hard	*5* a	*6* ɑ
forty	*8* ɔ	*20* ɔə
four	*9* o	
poor	*11* u	*21* ʊə

Table 5:2

Although there are no new items in the Scotland column, many more *different* items appear there than in the England column—nine (or ten if *4a* is included) as against six (or five if *20* falls together with *8*). It is noticeable that Scottish Standard English can make four distinctions corresponding to the single Anglo-English item *17*. Any modifications which may be made to the Scottish system towards the Anglo-English one are likely, therefore, in this restricted context /Vr/, to be in the direction of reducing rather than increasing the number of items. However, before discussing such possible modifications, we must note others which are consequent on two of the modifications to the Basic System already mentioned when Table 5:1 was being discussed.

The first is quite straightforward: if a distinction is made between *5* and *6*, then in this particular context *5* will be replaced in all cases by *6*.

The second is somewhat unexpected: if a distinction is made between *7* and *8*, then in this particular context *8* is likely to be replaced by *7*—a move *away* from the Anglo-English system, and one which gives rise to fairly conspicuous distribution differences. The use of *7* in *forty, border, short*, for example, is very noticeable to English ears. The reason for it may be that Scottish speakers who have a *7/8* distinction preserve, at the same time, vowel *9* in, for example, *four, boarder, court*; the use of *7* in the context /Vr/ ensures maximum differentiation. (Vowel *9* in this context may be heard also, in more or less the same words, in the rhotic accents of the West of England.)

The other modifications to the Basic Vowel System have no repercussions on this sub-system. There are, however, possible modifications to it which are not consequent on modifications to the Basic System.

The first of these is the replacement of *2* by *12*: the two, in this context, fall together. This modification may be heard from speakers with the Basic Vowel System, or with any modification to it. It could, I suppose, be said to be a modification towards the Anglo-English system in so far as it reduces by one the number of distinctions at this point.

The second, a more radical modification, is the complete loss of the distinctions between *2*, *12* and *4* (and also *4a*, if the speaker has it in his system). They all fall together in a true central vowel, which must be reckoned a further addition to the Scottish system, to be identified as *17* (although it differs from the Anglo-English *17* in being 'r-coloured', or pronounced with accompanying retroflexion). This reduction of the /Vr/ system seems never to be heard from speakers who otherwise use the Basic System; it always accompanies other modifications to the system. It is commonly heard from members of the professional classes in Edinburgh, Glasgow and other towns, and it appears to be on the increase. It clearly is one more modification towards the England system, even though, because of the 'r-colouring', the speaker must be considered to remain rhotic. (In fact rhoticity is maintained through all these modifications.)

We have so far been speaking of vowels in stressed syllables. Table 5:3 sets out typical vowels of unstressed syllables, which may be considered to form another sub-system (although many other vowels beside these are found in unstressed syllables, in both Scottish English and Anglo-English).

	Scotland	England
china	*12* ʌ	*22* ɔ
father	*2* ι	
pitted		*2* ι
pitied	*3* e	

Table 5:3

As in Table 5:2, Scotland has more items than England has: three as against two. There are no new items under Scotland, but there is one, number *22*, under England. This vowel completes the full inventory of Anglo-English vowels.

Two possible modifications to this Scottish sub-system of unstressed vowels should be noted. The first of these is a regional one: the replacement, in the north-east of Scotland, of *3* by *1*.

The second is the replacement of *2*, when followed by /r/, by an 'r-coloured' central vowel which may be identified with *22*, adding yet another possible item to a maximum Scottish vowel system. This is a modification which goes with the addition to a vowel system of *17*: the one implies the other.

Another possible change in Scottish English vowels which modifies them in the direction of Anglo-English is the use of diphthongs instead of monophthongs for vowels *3* and *9*. This is not common, and of course such a change does not make any difference to the system, but merely to the realisation of items in the system.

There is thus a much wider variety of vowel systems in Standard English in Scotland than in England. The Basic System, with thirteen items, is a remarkably small system for Standard English; as far as I am aware, it is the smallest vowel system in the English-speaking world.

I have space to deal only briefly with the remaining characteristics of Scottish Standard English, including the 'non-segmental' features of intonation, voice quality, and rhythm, on which, as I said at the beginning, much work remains to be done.

Intonation is very varied among Standard English accents in Scotland, almost certainly more varied than in England. There are probably bigger intonation differences to be found between, for instance, Edinburgh and Glasgow, which are only fifty miles or so apart, than within the whole of England. There has, however, been relatively little investigation of such variations. People have tended to fight shy of the study, as it is certainly a difficult subject.

Rhythm is another feature where accents may differ from each other. All accents of Standard English are spoken with what is known as a *stress-timed* rhythm, which means that the stressed, or salient, syllables tend to recur at roughly equal intervals of time, i.e. to be 'isochronous', as distinct from the *syllable-timed* rhythm of many other languages, where all the *syllables* are isochronous and recur at roughly equal intervals of time. (Not all *dialects* of English are stress-timed.

Syllable-timed types of English are found in the West Indies, for example, and West African Pidgin—if indeed it is a kind of English—is syllable-timed.)

However, although all Standard English accents have a stress-timed rhythm, they are not all the same in their rhythmic details, and there is one characteristic of the rhythm of Scottish speech which, once attention is drawn to it, is very noticeable. It is one which I have not come across in any other accent of Standard English. It concerns syllable *quantity* or length. Let me give an example. When I, as one type of speaker from England, say a two-syllable word such as *table*, I give roughly equal length to each of the two syllables. A Yorkshire speaker, on the other hand, will say the word with a long first syllable and a short second syllable; so will a Cockney speaker. Most accents of Standard English have either this equal–equal or this long–short relationship between the two syllables. In Scotland, however, one finds a relationship between the two syllable-lengths which is unusual: the first syllable is short and the second is long. There is, curiously enough, an interesting parallel to this in Scottish music; it is known as the 'Scottish snap', which is typical of strathspeys and is found in many songs. I cannot help feeling there must be some connexion between the occurrence of these two rhythmic facts in those different fields.

Another point might be mentioned while on the subject of syllables. Most accents of Standard English use syllable *division* to distinguish meanings, making clear the difference between, for example, *a name* and *an aim*. Scots are much less inclined to use such differences for this purpose. In fact there is much more regularity about syllable division in Scots than elsewhere in English. Scottish speakers make as many syllables *open* syllables as possible (an open syllable is one that ends in a vowel), so that they will attach the final consonant of a word to the beginning of the next word, if it starts with a vowel. Thus they would not distinguish between *a name* and *an aim*: in both cases the *n* would belong to the second syllable. This could be put another way, rather more technically, by saying that in Scots a consonant is made a releasing consonant in a syllable when it is possible to do so. This is uncommon (though not unknown) in other types of English, but it would be the usual thing in some other languages such as French. Thus I constantly hear people say *Sn-tAndrews* for what I would call

Snt-Andrews (using a hyphen to indicate the syllable division). (We know that *tawdry* comes from *St Audrey*, though this is hardly likely to be due to Scottish influence.) *Voice quality* is another aspect of speech which is difficult to investigate and therefore neglected. Scottish accents of Standard English have voice qualities which are characteristic of them and different from other accents of Standard English; I recognise this when I listen to them, but I find myself unable to say precisely in what the characteristic qualities consist, or even to find adequate descriptive labels for them. The great phonetician Henry Sweet (himself half Scots) claimed that there was a kind of Scottish voice quality familiarly known as 'the pig's whistle'; he attributed the effect to narrowing of the upper glottis or ventricular bands. I have not myself succeeded in identifying the pig's whistle among Scottish speakers, and the expression seems to have fallen into disuse, at any rate in this sense. Some very interesting work on voice quality, however, is being done at the moment in the Department of Linguistics at Edinburgh, which we hope will throw light on the problem of describing and classifying voice qualities in general, and of identifying those which are associated with Scots, and which appear to vary both with region and with social class.

Finally, brief mention might be made of *weak forms*, as they are called: forms of certain words such as prepositions, pronouns and others, which come into use when these words are not stressed. They are found in connected speech in all kinds of English. Their occurrence is *syntactically* determined in most Standard English accents: clear rules can be given to describe their use, rules which mostly do not have exceptions. In Scottish, however, perhaps alone among accents of Standard English, weak forms are *stylistically* rather than syntactically determined: their occurrence depends almost entirely on the speed of talking and on the formality of the occasion. But in any case weak forms are less common in connected speech in Scotland than the rest of the English-speaking world, although at the same time more words have weak forms in Scottish Standard English than elsewhere: *on*, for example, has no weak form in Anglo-English but it has in Scotland.

Is there anything to be said in general phonetic terms about Scottish Standard English? I think it can, briefly, be characterised as efficient, frugal, and straightforward. It is efficient in being highly intelligible on an international scale. It is frugal systemically: it has a vowel system which does what is needed, with no frills, although it allows itself one small luxury in the consonant system—the voiceless velar fricative—which gives it, perhaps, a touch of distinction. It is straightforward structurally, being rhotic, and does not get involved in such complex matters as linking and intrusive /r/s. It is interesting that it conforms very well to what could be called 'Standard Average European' phonology; many accents of England, particularly RP, are extremely aberrant from European norms.

Because of these things Scottish Standard English provides a very good model of pronunciation for foreign learners of English, particularly since it also escapes the political associations that go with RP and with 'General American', the models that are usually taught.

In conclusion I should like to repeat that these remarks on Scottish Standard English are based on the analysis of the accents of about five hundred Scottish students at Edinburgh University, over the last quarter of a century. I think these students provide a fair sample of Lowland Scottish speakers. For a number of years now nothing very much that is new has cropped up in the way of segmental features. We need, as can be seen, much more investigation of non-segmental features if a phonological description of Scottish Standard English is to rank equal with descriptions of what is most unjustifiably widely referred to as 'British English', which is what the English (and Americans!) call RP.

1   There is further discussion of this phenomenon in Chapter 6 (p 101); see also note 9.

6
Scottish Speech:
a historical view with special reference to the Standard English of Scotland
A J Aitken

A Model of Scottish Speech
I want to begin by establishing a model of current Scots speech, which is set out in Table 6:1 on the following page. The table is intended to display macrocosmically the range of speech options actually in use among all the different groups of Lowland Scots speakers, and also microcosmically the range of alternatives theoretically available to individual speakers. Macrocosmically it offers a behaviourist view of the observed actions of speakers generally, microcosmically it represents the competence of individual Scottish speakers. The labels 'Scots' and 'English' are among those commonly applied by Scots to the contents of the columns above which they are placed; they also designate quite accurately the historical origins of the different sets of options. Columns 1 and 2 derive historically from earlier native Scots speech; columns 4 and 5 represent later importations from southern English; and much of the vocabulary and grammar part of column 3 consists of material which has since the outset been common ground between these two dialects. The two components—Scots and English—together make up the composite 'Scots English' of Dr McArthur's Chapter 4.

One statement that the model would permit us to make is that individual Scottish speakers may choose to speak fairly exclusively from columns 1 to 3 of Table 6:1 (when they do, they are often said to be 'speaking Scots' or 'speaking very broad' or 'speaking very broad dialect') or exclusively from columns 3 to 5 (in Scotland, this is usually called 'speaking English'). It is this last sort of speech with which we are mainly concerned in this part of the book. Between these extremes there are all sorts of intermediate possibilities, for example, occasionally drawing material from 4 and 5 in a form of speech based mainly on columns 1 to 3, and conversely. Many Scots speakers also operate the Scots and English bases as different registers, using one or the other under different social circumstances. Some such speakers can

————Scots————			————English————	
1	*2*	*3*	*4*	*5*
bairn	mair	before	more	child
lass	stane		stone	girl
kirk	hame	name	home	church
chaft	dee	see	die	jaw
gowpen	heid	tie	head	double handful
ken	hoose	tide	house	know
bide	loose (*n*)	young	louse (*n*)	remain
kenspeckle	louse (*adj*)	winter	loose (*adj*)	conspicuous
low	yaize (*v*)	of	use (*v*)	flame
cowp	yis (*n*)	is	use (*n*)	capsize
shauchle	auld	some	old	shuffle
whae's aucht that?	truith	why	truth	whose is that?
pit the haims on	barra	he	barrow	do in
tummle wulkies		they		turn somersaults
no (*adv*)		*		not (*adv*)
-na (*adv*)		†		-n't (*adv*)

*(*Most of the inflectional system, word-order grammar.*)
†(*Pronunciation system and rules of realisation.*)

Table 6:1

switch quite cleanly from one to the other—these people have been called *dialect-switchers*. Others again either cannot or do not choose to control their styles in this way, but they do shift styles in a less predictable and more fluctuating way—these people we may call *style-drifters*. The actual practice of such speakers is governed by the expectation that the higher social status of particular speakers or the greater formality of style of any speaker is normally accompanied by a shift towards the English pole of the system. Of course one could say a lot more about these phenomena, noting, for example, that the system is somewhat polarised: there is a general tendency to associate Scots expressions with other Scots expressions and English expressions with other English expressions and some juxtapositions of items across the system are probably disallowed. However, this will serve for our present purposes.[1]

One thing we *can* say about this situation is that it is very different from the situation of Scottish speech as this existed in Scotland down to the sixteenth century. At that time the English options (columns 4 and 5 of Table 6:1) were not available at all to Scottish speakers (though some were to writers of Scottish poetry) and *their* stylistic variations had to be managed within the resources of columns 1 to 3.

The Historical Setting

In the sixteenth century Scots was still fairly autonomous of southern English (more strictly, see below, Midland and South-Eastern English; in this paper I shall use as cover terms 'southern English' or, if no ambiguity seems likely, simply 'English'). At that time two nations shared this island, each with its own distinct national tongue, King's Scots in Scotland and King's English in England. Distinct, but closely related and in many respects identical, national tongues, otherwise the later merger into a single composite system could not have taken place. In other words, though the two languages were in a political or social sense separate languages, in a linguistic sense they were distinct but related dialects, much as is the case with the Scandinavian languages today.

In a simple way this relationship is expressed by the following family tree:

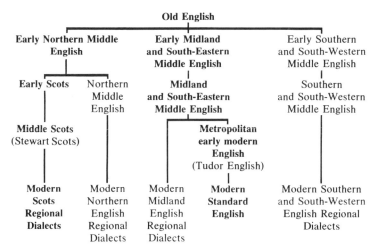

Figure 6:1

As Figure 6:1 shows, sixteenth-century Stewart Scots and metropolitan Tudor English had Old English (or Anglo-Saxon, the language of the Anglian and Saxon peoples of pre-

Norman Britain) as their common ancestor. In the figure the vertical axis represents the time dimension and the horizontal one the spatial dimension—except, of course, that Standard English is no longer (as it was down to the sixteenth century) local to south-eastern England. It has since then been carried to, or adopted in, every part of the English-speaking world, including Scotland: it is now the language discussed by Tom McArthur in Chapter 4 of this book as 'World Standard English'. Within Scotland, this World Standard English in its local manifestation as Scottish Standard English has merged since the sixteenth century with the native non-standard Scots dialect speech (labelled Modern Scots Regional Dialects in Figure 6:1), and the result of this merger is the composite system discussed in the previous section.

I want now to sketch in some of the events which led to the enlargement, or, we might say, anglicisation, of the simpler, sixteenth-century, exclusively Scottish system into the composite one we have today. I shall be concentrating mainly on external events—on political and social changes which influenced the development of the system. I have no room either to specify the numerous obvious ways in which sixteenth-century Scots differed from Tudor English (though many of these are reflected in peculiarities of later Scots and Scottish Standard English, and we will meet them later) or to give more than a couple of sentences to the *internal* history of Scots since the sixteenth century. In part this internal history proceeded on lines common to all varieties of English, including, for example, the development of new periphrastic negative and interrogative constructions—*he cums nocht* becoming *he's no cumin, he cam nocht* becoming *he didna cum*. On the other hand, some further developments affected particular Scots dialects only, and many new Scotticisms of vocabulary have appeared since the sixteenth century.

One other trend which can be demonstrated, albeit most commentators on the history of Scots presume merely to take it for granted, is a slow attrition of distinctively Scots elements in the system and their replacement in more recent times by corresponding Standard English forms. Thus items from columns 1 and 2 of Table 6:1 disappear and column 3 is correspondingly enlarged by items formerly from columns 4 and 5—items like, say, *icker* – an *ear* of corn or, in many dialects, *lift* – the *sky* or *aik* – an *oak* or, in some dialects at least, *bate* – a *boat* or *aits* – *oats*. This, then, reduces the

Scottishness of the system. But it is a very long way from anglicising it totally, as we can see by looking at the writings of any of our modern writers in the 'stairheid vernacular'.

I have suggested that one enabling factor in the anglicising of late medieval Scots was the partial identity of Scots and (Midland and South-Eastern) English as closely related dialects in the linguistic sense. Because of this, elements originally English could be infiltrated into Scots writings and, later, speech, without appearing too incongruous. Another conditioning factor was the evident lack in fifteenth-, sixteenth- and seventeenth-century Scotland of any general feeling of strong linguistic loyalty (though some individuals apparently had this). Consequently, there were no great patriotic objections to an infiltration of first written, and later spoken, Scots by usages of English origin. There are indeed various indications that, at least as early as the sixteenth century, Scots, albeit the national tongue, was nevertheless widely felt to be less suited to the most dignified kinds of writing—being a homely, domestic, maternal language—than Tudor English was. A quite explicit statement of this view is that of Sir William Alexander, one of the self-styled 'Scoto-Britanes' who followed James VI to London after 1603:

> The language of this Poeme is (as thou seest) mixt of the English and Scottish Dialects; which perhaps may be un-pleasant and irksome to some readers of both nations. But I hope the gentle and Judicious Englishe reader will beare with me, if I retaine some badge of mine owne countrie, by using sometimes words that are peculiar thereunto, especiallie when I finde them propre, and significant. And as for my owne countrymen, they may not justly finde fault with me, if for the more parte I vse the English phrase, as worthie to be preferred before our owne for the elegance and perfection thereof. Yea I am perswaded that both countrie-men will take in good part the mixture of their Dialects, the rather for that the bountiful providence of God doth invite them both to a straiter union and conjunction as well in language, as in other respects. (Sir William Alexander: *Darius*, To the Reader (1603) in L E Kastner & H B Charlton (eds), *The Poetical Works of Sir William Alexander Earl of Stirling*, (Edinburgh: Scottish Text Society, 1921), vol 1 p cxcvi.)

Sir William pretends to use a 'mixed' language and indeed does retain a sprinkling of Scotticisms in the text of this play and his other earlier works (though he then set about gradually weeding out these Scotticisms in subsequent editions of his works). But it is clear enough where his heart really is, and what he writes here can scarcely be called anything but English. Although, as a result of the superior prestige of English literature and the English predilections of the Scottish reformers, and partly in anticipation of the Union of the Crowns, an intermittent and variable anglicisation of the spellings of Scottish writings had been proceeding through the sixteenth century, most Scottish texts of this time are however nothing like as anglicised as this of Sir William Alexander's. As a specimen of *Scots* of the late sixteenth century we may look at this passage:

> Lawes nather throwlie weill maid for punishment of sic hynous crymes, and manie weill maid wantes execution, lyk athercape wobbes that taks the sillie flies, bot the bumbarts braks throw tham! Be the insatiable sacrilegius avarice of Erles, Lords, and Gentlemen, the Kirk, Scholles, and Pure, ar spulyied of that quhilk sould sustein tham. The materiall Kirks lyes lyk sheipe and nout faulds rather than places of Christian congregationes to assemble into. The parochinars will haiff a couple of skores of hirdes for thair cattell, bot skarse a Pastor to feid thrie thowsand of thair saulles. (James Melvill, *Autobiography and Diary*, (London: Wodrow Society, 1842), p 188. From a document of 1584.)

The one anglicised form in this passage is *manie* in line 2 (the native Scottish form was *mony*), and the one non-Scots spelling symbol is <sh> in <punishment> and <sheipe> (traditionally Scots had preferred <sch>).

But though Scottish *writing* was certainly becoming anglicised in the sixteenth century and continued further in the same direction in the seventeenth, the indications are that, except for a very few Scotsmen of unusual personal histories like John Knox, the *speech* of all Scotsmen continued fully Scots into the seventeenth century.

However, following the Scottish Reformation in 1560, Scotsmen of all classes were coming for the first time into regular visual and aural contact with writings in southern English: aural in that at least once a week, and in the case of devout people several times a week, they heard readings from the Bible in southern English, and sermons in a language partly modelled on Biblical English. One of the crucial facts in the history of Scots is that it never had its own translation of the Bible, and that Scottish worshippers of this time sang from an English Psalter.

And in the course of the seventeenth century there was a considerable increase in face-to-face contacts between Scotsmen and Englishmen. Now we had the 'Scoto-Britanes'. What seems to be a suggestion that those Scots lairds who sold up land to support them on fortune-seeking visits to London anglicised their speech as well as their manners comes from William Lithgow in 1633. In his 'Scotland's Welcome to King Charles' (in Lithgow, *Poeticall Remains*, (1863), p 94) he writes of these emigrants:

> Whose *Riggs* speake *English* & their falted *furres*
> Forgetting *Scots* can *speek* with gilded spurres.

The English troops who garrisoned Scotland in the 1650s may well have exercised some linguistic influence also. But no doubt most important of all these linguistic anglicising influences was the great increase which occurred in this century in contacts of all sorts between the landed gentry of Scotland and landed and wealthy English people.

From this time onwards intermarriage between the Scots and English aristocracies became common. It has been calculated that 13.7 per cent, or 62 out of 454, of seventeenth-century Scots peers contracted marriages with wives from south of the Border (chiefly English, though six were Welshwomen), though of these women only 23 were from the aristocracy, many of the remainder including wealth rather than noble birth among their attractions. This was a trend which, almost unknown before 1603, increased towards the end of the century: 'London was becoming a marriage market for Scotland as well as for England'. On the other hand the percentage of daughters of Scottish peers who married out of their own nation and class was very much smaller (28 out of 826, or 3.39 per cent)[2]. After the Restoration, every Scotsman of the nobility was likely to spend part of his time in southern England, at court or residing in the Home Counties, and nearly all other eminent Scots—let us say those who get into the *Dictionary of National Biography*—visited London for shorter or longer periods.[3] Although the practice among well-

to-do Scots of sending their sons to school in England—
pioneered by John Knox in the sixteenth century—seems to
have remained uncommon till the late eighteenth century, it
was not entirely unknown at this time.[4]

Under these circumstances it would not be too surprising
if the Scottish upper classes, socially southernised in this
way, had also given up their native Scots speech for the more
'elegant and perfect' English of the south. A study of the
spellings and vocabulary of the private correspondence of
Scots county families during the seventeenth century would
support this assumption.

It is, of course, possible to write in a way that belies how
one speaks, but there are a number of indications that the
hybrid written language of the seventeenth-century Scottish
gentry's private correspondence genuinely reflects a rapidly
anglicising, mixed kind of speech. One bit of evidence of this
kind is this passage:

> We cannot forgett also a note of a ministers (called Mr.
> Rob. Vedderburne) preaching related me by Robert
> Scot which happened besyde them. God will even
> come over the hil at the back of the kirk their, and cry
> wt a hy woice, Angel of the church of Malnmoonsy,
> compeir; than Ile answer, Lord, behold thy servant
> what hes thou to say to him. Then God wil say, Wheir
> are the souls thou hest won by your ministery heir thir
> 17 years? Ile no wal what to answer to this, for, Sirs, I
> cannot promise God one of your souls: yet Ile say,
> behold my own Soul and my crooked Bessies (this was
> his daughter), and will not this be a sad matter? (John
> Lauder of Fountainhall, *Journals*, SHS 36, 1900, p 54.)

Notice that God and the minister conduct their dialogue in
Biblical English, though at one point God 'faws through it'
with *thir 17 years*. But the form of most interest in the
passage is *no* in *Ile no wal* (I'll know well). The point is that
this must be a phonetic spelling for the English spoken form
know: it cannot represent the Scottish equivalents *knaw* or
ken. Similar phonetic spellings of forms with underlying
South-Eastern English pronunciations appear in other writings by Scots in seventeenth-century Scotland: *towe, tow*
(=two, in place of Scots *twa* or *twae*)—1610 *Inventory* of
Lord Bruce of Kinloss, another of the 'Scoto-Britanes' (in
Ferrerii Historia Abbatum de Kynlos (Bannatyne Club, 1839)

p xi); *wan, tow* (=one, two; in place of Scots *ane, twa* or *twae*)—1652 *Atholl Papers* (in *Aberdeen University Review* **36**, p 191); *how* (=who; in place of Scots *wha* or *whae*)—1654 (in *Ane Account of the Familie of Innes* (Spalding Club, 1864) p 175); *tu* (=two)—1657 (in *The Records of Elgin* (New Spalding Club, 1903) p 302).

In this way, it seems, the speech of the Scots gentry assimilated to polite southern English in the course of the seventeenth century. The choice of word-forms and vocabulary in their private correspondence seems to suggest that their speech passed through a stage when there was rather inconsistent vacillation between native and imported southern options in these respects—such as we get from working-class Scots 'style-drifters' today—to a variety which fairly consistently preferred southern English forms and words. The phonetic realisation of this anglicised dialect is of course another matter: the *accent* with which the Scots realised their southern English may well have remained markedly Scottish; and indeed there are suggestions (see p 95) that it did.

It is doubtless possible to exaggerate the length things had gone by the early eighteenth century. Further movement towards the adoption of 'Southern gnaps' (see note 6) was still to come. And individuals no doubt varied, as they do today. But the overall impression must be that the sixteenth-century situation in which all Scots—with very rare exceptions like John Knox—simply spoke native Older Scots had been superseded by a new situation. In this new situation the formal or, in the language of the time, 'polite' speech of the social élite of Scotland was now expected to approximate to the southern English dialect represented in columns 3 to 5 in Table 6:1. This was now the language of people with social pretensions and for discussing intellectual topics or speaking in formal circumstances. For some it must also have already become the usual informal or fully vernacular style. And a form of speech which mostly favoured traditional Scots usages (as in columns 1 and 2 of the Table) was now identified with conservatives, eccentrics and, especially, 'the common people' or 'the vulgar'.

This, at any rate, seems to have been the situation in the mind of Sir Robert Sibbald when, in 1710, he distinguishes between three different varieties of Scots speech: 'The Language of the common People' or 'that Language we call Broad Scots, which is yet used by the Vulgar', 'in distinction to the *Highlanders* Language, and the refined Language of the Gentry, which the more Polite People among us do use, and is made up of *Saxon, French* and *Latin* Words'. (*The History of the Sheriffdoms of Fife and Kinross* (Edinburgh, 1710) pp 15; 16.) 'The refined Language of the Gentry', we must presume, approximated to the language Sir Robert wrote—it was a variety of southern (or Standard) English.

That the horror of lexical and idiomatic Scotticisms which was to haunt the Scottish intelligentsia through much of the eighteenth century was already part of the linguistic consciousness of educated Scots by the end of the seventeenth, we may infer from the following. First, that the use of Scottish words and locutions contributed to the ludicrousness which Scottish Episcopalians ascribed to the sermons and some other writings of seventeenth-century Presbyterian preachers (see *The Scotch Presbyterian Eloquence* (London, 1692) pp 89ff). Second, the Presbyterians themselves were touchy on this point:

> And certainly no Scots Man can approve our Authors ridiculing his own Country Language, or impute it as a Crime in Mr *Rutherford*, to use the meanest Phrase to make himself the better understood by those he wrote to; which shows his Humility and Condescension, that he could *cum balbutiensibus balbutire*, so he might gain them to Christ, a drudgery apparently below the Genius of our pretended Seraphick Prelatists.... Neither was ever Mr *Rutherford's* Letters designed to the Press by himself, but those who had them, finding their usefulness to themselves, thought they could not but be acceptable to the Publick, though in a homely Stile, there being none of the Sentences which our Author ridicules, but what are highly significant in our Dialect. And this may serve for an Answer to the Notes of other Sermons which they expose, because of Scotisms. (*An Answer to the Scotch Presbyterian Eloquence* (London, 1693) p 57.)

And there are other indications that some Scots were now anxious to eliminate Scotticisms from their speech:

> You know I came to *England* the last time upon no other account, but to learn the Language, and promised to keep correspondence with you upon this condition, that you would make remarks upon my Letters,

and faithfully Admonish me of all the Scoticisms, or all
the Words, and Phrases that are not current *English*
therein. I confess I have a great Veneration for our
own and the Northern *English* Language, upon the
account of the Anglo-Saxon, to which they are so
nearly ally'd; but yet... am as ambitious to write
modern *English*, as any Gascon, or Provencal can be
to write the modern French. (*Ravillac Redivivus*
(London, 1678) p 77.)

So we may assume that as a dialect—in its word-forms and
words—the new 'refined language of the gentry' of Scotland
approximated to Standard English by about the time of the
Revolution and of the Union of Parliaments, albeit this
'refined language' was occasionally marred by a lexical Scotticism or two. But what about its pronunciation, the precise
manner in which the individual sounds of which it was made
up were realised, and other features of 'accent', such as
rhythm and intonation features? On this, an English visitor to
Scotland of 1689 (Rev Thomas Morer) says the following:

They have an unhappy tone, which the gentry and
nobles cannot overcome, tho' educated in our schools,
or never so conversant with us; so that we may dis-
cover a Scotchman as soon as we hear him speak: Yet
to say truth, our Northern and remote English have the
same imperfection. (From P Hume Brown, *Early
Travellers in Scotland* (Edinburgh, 1891) pp 272–273.)

So some Scots of the upper and middle classes still used
occasional Scotticisms, though uneasily aware that these
were regarded as undignified and associated with 'the common people', and they spoke their English with a noticeable
Scottish accent. However, this was just at the time when the
Augustan culture of eighteenth-century England was strongly
influencing the Scottish cultural scene. And Augustanism was
a fashion which laid great emphasis on 'propriety' and pro-
hibited in 'polite' usage anything 'unrefined', 'vulgar' or 'provincial' (by the standards of upper-class London, that is).

These prescriptions were swallowed by nearly all the
educated Scots of the eighteenth century, though there were
some dissentient voices like those of the poets Allan Ramsay[5]
and Alexander Ross.[6] A notable result was a greatly increased
self-consciousness of the Scots intellectuals and middle classes about the provinciality of their English speech. Residual

Scottish features were now regarded as sullying what might otherwise have been exemplary refined English, and it was all but universally accepted as desirable for anyone with pretensions to being 'polite' that he should write and speak English with 'propriety'—that is, according to the standards of London society. This is already in evidence in the records of the Fair Intellectual Club, founded in 1719 for educated young ladies of Edinburgh, in which the first president complimented her members on the propriety of their English 'considering how difficult it is for our country people to acquire it'. The well-known consequences of these notions include the publication, from 1752 onwards, of several alphabetical lists of Scottish words and expressions, compiled expressly so that Scots people could learn to avoid them in their writing and speech, and the descent on Edinburgh, from 1748 onwards, of a long line of English, Irish and anglicised Scottish lecturers on elocution, spearheading the attack on the Scots accent.[7]

Alas, these earnest efforts of our ancestors had only very limited effect, as my own speech and that of many other middle-class Scots of today testifies. It is possible to point to certain lexical Scotticisms, like *to come,* or *sit, into the fire,* the past participle form *proven,* the verb *evite,* which seem to have been successfully eliminated. But as many or more others, equally subject to overt condemnation by the eighteenth-century and later compilers of lists of Scotticisms, are still very much with us—such as *angry at, tomorrow forenoon, the length of* (=as far as), and *ill to guide.*

I shall be suggesting below that some of the features which differentiate the accents of present-day middle-class Scots from those of working-class Scottish speakers were introduced on an English model at this time. In many other ways, however, the middle-class Scottish accent remains very evidently Scottish, as we shall see.

To us, these attempts of our eighteenth-century ancestors at finally purifying middle-class Scottish speech of Scotticism and Scottishness may seem very limited in their success. At the time they must have seemed more successful. Around 1785 the extreme self-consciousness and the strident note of linguistic insecurity which mark the middle years of the century die out. Some of the remarks we read thereafter, especially those directed towards a new aim, that of totally extirpating the continuing broad Scots of the lower orders, which was now regarded as 'a mass of perfect and absurd corruption' (J G Dalyell, *Scotish Poems, of the Sixteenth Century* (1801) p x), are in tones which imply the complete confidence of the writers themselves in the propriety of their own English. There are many of these. Here, as a single example, is how the minister of Peterhead writes of the language of his parishioners in 1795:

> The language spoken in this parish is the broad Buchan dialect of the English, with many Scotticisms, and stands much in need of reformation, which it is hoped will soon happen, from the frequent resort of polite people to the town in summer. (*The Statistical Account of Scotland*, 1795, 'Peterhead'.)

Though some continued, and continue no doubt today, to hold that the total extinction of vernacular Scots is desirable, this seems to have ceased to be the establishment position early in the nineteenth century. We may perhaps associate this change of heart with the publication of Jamieson's Dictionary in 1808, with the new wave of Scots Romantic writers, with the burgeoning of nineteenth-century antiquarianism and with the sturdy Scots patriotism of people like Lord Cockburn. It was now accepted that Scots was 'going out as a spoken tongue every year' but for some, such as Cockburn in 1838, this was a matter for nostalgic regret at the incipient demise of a rich and expressive old tongue and no longer, as it had been, for universal congratulation. (*Journal of Henry Cockburn 1831–1854*, I (Edinburgh, 1874), p 189.)

The following passage sums up some of the linguistic and linguistic-mythological conditions and attitudes to which the foregoing events had led:

> Among the higher and better educated classes the English language may be heard spoken in tolerable purity both as to idiom and pronunciation: there are few who cannot express themselves in English, still fewer who do not familiarly understand it when spoken to them. Unmixed Scotch is never to be heard. The most common dialect is a mixture of Scotch and English, the Scotch used being of the somewhat vicious kind, known, I believe, by the name of the Aberdeenshire. The Scotch, however, is gradually wearing out. Every person remembers the frequent use, in former years, of terms and phrases that are now seldom to be heard but among the older and more

secluded. Even however in what is called by courtesy
speaking English or using English words there is often
a sore lack of the genuine English pronunciation. (*The
Second Statistical Account of Scotland*, 1845, 'Banff'.)

Until this time only two kinds of language had been named as
potential claimants for the allegiance of (Lowland) Scottish
speakers—'English' and 'Scotch'. Now, however, we begin to
meet a more selective approach to value-judgements of
'Scotch' itself. About 1840 Andrew Crawfurd avers that the
influx of 'a clanjamfray of Irish, Highlanders and other
dyvours' into the village of Lochwinnoch, Renfrewshire, has
brought in 'a Babylonish dialect, both in idioms and in accent'. He adds, however, that 'this corruption is alone in the
village . . . The country part of the parish exhibits a pattern
approaching to the Doric and chaste dialect.' (*Crawfurd MSS*,
c 1840, Paisley Library.) In the year 1901 we meet several
arraignments of a certain 'wonderful gibberish which now
passes current for Scotch', marked by forms like *be-a* for
better and *wa-a* for *water* (i.e. presumably, by the realisation
of intervocalic *t* as a glottal stop), the syncretism of past tense
and past participle forms of certain verbs (*if he hadnae
went, . . . he wad hae fell*) and other shibboleths with which
we are still familiar, and designated 'Glasgow-Irish'. (R de B
Trotter, 'The Scottish Language' in *The Gallovidian* 3, 1901,
pp 22–24.) In the same year (1901) this variety is joined in the
dock by a variety described as 'the "Keelveensoide" patois of
the West-end of Glasgow'. (D McNaught, 'The raucle tongue
of Burns' in *Annual Burns Chronicle* 10, 1901, pp 26–37.)
However, these are merely 'corruptions' of Scots or English,
as all three of these writers are agreed. 'The Doric and chaste
dialect', the 'Scotch language' still surviving in 'the smaller
villages and rural districts' is of course perfectly acceptable
to these writers, though believed to be 'as good as dead'.

In somewhat more recent times the approvable forms of
Scottish speech are held to include (I quote from a Scottish
Education Department report of 1952) on the one hand 'an
exemplar of English generally acceptable to educated Scots'
and on the other 'words and phrases of genuine dialect,
whether of the Borders or of Buchan' which, says the document, 'should find a place in the classroom'. Conversely,
however, the report expresses the hope that 'slovenly perversions of dialect will . . . be excluded'. (*English in Secondary*

Schools (Edinburgh: Scottish Education Dept, 1952) p 6.) This view of Scottish speech, with its threefold classification into 'educated' Scottish Standard English (approvable), 'genuine dialect' (approvable) and 'corruptions of dialect' or 'slovenly perversions of dialect' (not approvable), has held sway among those Scots who concerned themselves at all with such matters until quite recently. The challenge which it is now meeting from linguists and some other writers is still resisted by many, both among the establishment and at other levels of Scottish society.

The 'Educated' Scottish Accent: survivals and innovations
Where does this place the English-based variety of Scottish speech, that based mainly on columns 3 to 5 of Table 6:1 and the variety with which we are specially concerned in this section of the book? Where lie the origins of the Scottish peculiarities of the 'Basic' system of 'educated' Scottish Standard English described by Professor Abercrombie in Chapter 5 (pp 72–75) and other peculiarities of this variety to be mentioned below? Obviously enough, though the dialect in which they are manifested originated in southern England and reached Scotland by way of imitation of this extraneous English dialect by seventeenth- and eighteenth-century Scots, practically all the *special* features of this variety belong to the older native part of our speech tradition and were originally associated with native *Scots* speech. They result from the prolonged contact of the two sides of Scottish speech-tradition, often in the speech-practice of single individuals, who dialect-switch from Scots to English or style-drift across the range of Scottish speech. The presence of speakers like this has always been part of the Scottish linguistic scene: noteworthy instances were Robert Burns and no doubt many of the eighteenth-century literati, as well as Scots of a later generation like Scott, Hogg and Cockburn, and so on down to many of us today.

Essentially, what the anglicising Scots of the seventeenth, eighteenth and later centuries learned to do was to replace the distinctive and provincial native items of word-form, vocabulary and idiom and the more obtrusively native Scots rules of grammar, as in columns 1 and 2 of Table 6:1, with the corresponding material from columns 4 and 5. So they learned, at the level of *dialect*, a lot of new word-forms and new words. The books of instruction on usage and orthoepy (or

correct pronunciation) which were addressed to Scots anglicisers in the eighteenth century and later in reality offer only
prescriptions for *this* kind of change, along with some in-
structions for modifying the stress and vocalism patterns of
forms like *Apríle* or *committée* or *Júly*. What these books
fail to do is to teach the Scots how to reform their traditional pronunciation habits at the *accent* level into a
thoroughly southern English mould. Books alone could hardly
in any case be expected to achieve that kind of reform. The
only way to relearn one's pronunciation at that level is by
imitation of heard models. And though there is little doubt
that the eighteenth-century Scots literati wanted to do this,
that there was plenty of will in this direction, most of them
simply lacked adequate opportunity. A few lectures by
authorities on English pronunciation, occasional meetings
with English visitors, and occasional trips to London would
not accomplish this; though no doubt there were some, those
whose southern sojourns were longer or whose parents had
the foresight to send them to English schools, who did
better—like, we presume, James Boswell and others.[8] When
eventually, near the end of the eighteenth century, the Scots
gentry gained confidence in the propriety of their own brand
of English and, still more, with the nineteenth-century revival
of cultural patriotism, the motive for trying to ape English
speech-habits at this subtle level of accent was weakened,
though perhaps not entirely removed.

So it is that there continue in educated Scottish Standard
English many ancient accent features of doubtless native
Scots origin. These include habits of rhythm and intonation,
of the history of which we know very little, but which are
believed to be highly persistent over long stretches of time.
Differences between the educated Scottish and other English
systems of consonants and vowels mostly reflect the greater
conservatism of Scottish speech habits in these respects.
Among the consonants, Scots English has failed to merge *hw-*
and *w-* in *whales* and *Wales* and it has never abandoned the
distinctive consonant in *loch, clachan, Brechin*. As for the
vowels, the unusually small Scottish vowel-system—Professor Abercrombie's 'Basic System'—results from the fact that
Scots did not follow London English in the seventeenth and
eighteenth centuries in splitting its /u/ phoneme and its /a/
phoneme into two; also, seventeenth-century Scots dialects
possessed at most (some had none at all) only one low back

round vowel to serve as vowel number *8* in Professor Abercrombie's Table 5:1, whereas southern English already had
both *7* and *8*. The continuing 'rhoticism' (see p 69) of Scots
English is also a conservative feature. Here again Scots failed
to follow middle-class South-Eastern English of the late
seventeenth century, in vocalising its non-pre-vocalic /r/ and
compensating for this with new diphthongs (as in RP *fear*
[fɪə], *there* [ðɛə], *soar* [sɔə], *poor* [pʊə]). On the other hand
the fact that Scots keeps its /r/ also enables it to maintain
certain contrasts which other kinds of English have lost: for
example, between *soared* [soːrd], *sword* [sɔːrd] and *sawed*
[sɔːd], or between *porn* [pɔrn] and *pawn* [pɔn], and between
birth [bɪrθ], *earth* [ɛrθ], Perth [pɛrθ] and *worth* [wʌrθ].

The precise ways in which these consonants and vowels
are realised similarly belong more to the Scots than to the
English side of our speech-tradition—the very close Scottish
[i] sound, the monophthongal [e]'s and [o]'s, the fact that, for
most of us, our initial voiceless stops lack most of the
aspiration which the phonetic text-books prescribe for RP,
and so on (for other features, see Chapter 5, pp 70–71 and 82.

Perhaps the most interesting of these native Scots realisational features of the Scottish accents of Standard English is
the 'Scottish Vowel-length Rule'.[9] This is a very pervasive
and very characteristically Scottish rule, which governs the
exact realisations in different phonetic and morphemic
environments of certain Scots vowels (those which were long,
or non-high short, monophthongs in fourteenth-century
Scots). To some extent it affects all Scots dialects, including
those of Orkney and Shetland and Northern Ireland, though
not all dialects display it for all vowels in all the possible
environments. Among the effects which it predicts are the
oppositions in Scots and Scottish Standard English (briefly
mentioned by Professor Abercrombie on p 77) between such
pairs as *agreed* [ʌ'griːd] and *greed* [grid], or *brewed* [bruːd]
and *brood* [brud], and *tied* [taed] and *tide* [tʌid], as well as
between such items as *feline* ['fiːlʌin] and *feeling* ['filʊŋ] or
pylon ['paelɔn] and *piling* ['pʌilʊŋ]. The Rule also produces
the striking differences in vowel-length in Scots and Scottish
Standard English speech between, on the one hand, such
items as *deave* [diːv] (to annoy) and *dear* [diːr] and, on the
other, *deef* [dif] (deaf) and *deid* [did] (dead) or *deed* [did]
(deed); and it is responsible for the different vocalisms, in
Central Scots and other dialects, of *use* (verb), with the

voiced consonant, as [jeːz], and *use* (noun), with the voice-less consonant, as [jʊs] or of *moor*, in Central Scots [meːr], and *good*, in Central Scots [gʊd].[10]

In an incipient form this Rule can be shown to date from at least as early as the fifteenth century and it was evidently fully realised in something like its modern form before 1650. Thus it long antedates the main anglicising of Scottish speech. Yet most Scots speakers operate it in their everyday Standard English, as one of these provincial features which the eight-eenth-century anglicisers failed to eliminate.

But this is not the whole story, of course. Not everything escaped anglicisation. Some of the differences of which we are all aware between present day middle-class and working-class Scottish speech result from the refusal, one might say, of middle-class Scottish speakers to follow their working-class compatriots in certain recent innovations in pronun-ciation-habit, such as the notorious glottal stop feature or the fronted Central Scots pronunciation of the /u/ vowel in working-class speech in words like *room* [rʉm] or [rÿm] and *good* [gÿd] and *new* [njÿ]. In other respects however, it is working-class speech which is conservative and the middle-class variety which is progressive, i.e. the working-class speaker maintains the traditional Scots practice, whereas middle-class speech has innovated in an anglicising direction. Among these innovations are the few successes (if that is the right word) of the eighteenth-century anglicisers.

To exemplify: many Scots dialects had and still have only one vowel corresponding to the two English vowels in words like *cot* and *coat*, *clock* and *cloak* (vowels 7 and 9 in Professor Abercrombie's Table 5:1, p 72). This vowel is, and probably was, realised as a moderately close one, [o], so it resembled Anglo-English vowel 9 rather than vowel 7 in this respect.

But this is a very obvious difference between the systems of Scots and English, and it was readily identified as such by eighteenth-century Scots observers of Scotticism. Con-sequently, there are a number of eighteenth- and nineteenth-century anecdotes illustrating the comic aspects of the efforts made by genteel eighteenth-century Scots to learn to pronounce *some* of their own original vowel 9 words with vowel 8 of Table 5:1 (which for most or all of them repre-sented Anglo-English 7 and 8 both), while continuing to pronounce others with vowel 9, according to the English standard—that is, to learn to say *coachbox* but not *cotch-boax*.[11] By and large they succeeded, though some speakers of Scottish Standard English today disagree with most of us in the vocalisms of a few words like *afford* and *pork* and *important* and *port* and *mourn*, giving these as [ʌˈfɔrd] and [pɔrk] and [ʊmˈpɔrtn̩t] and [pɔrt] and [mɔrn̩] (vowel *8*) rather than [ʌˈford] and [pork] and [ʊmˈportn̩t] and [port] and [morn̩] (vowel *9*). Conversely there is disagreement about *ford*, either as (the apparently more common Scottish Standard English) [fɔrd] (vowel *8*) or (the minority) [ford] (vowel *9*). The trouble here is that the spelling fails to discriminate, as it does in other environments, between *8* (*cot*) and *9* (*coat*).

This is one triumph of eighteenth-century accent-anglicisation, that its practitioners learned to discriminate, more or less in conformity with general Standard English practice, between two sorts of *o* vowel. There were other achievements of a similar sort. Perhaps it was at this time that North-Eastern Scots speakers learned to say [ˈdɔtʊr ɪn ˈlɔː] in conformity with Central Scots and general middle-class British practice, rather than [ˈdaːtʊr ɪn ˈlaː], which was all that their native system allowed for in the range of vowel-realisations it contained.[12]

It seems most likely that the widespread modern Scots vernacular realisations of the phoneme /ɪ/ (in words like *sit* and *lid* and *hill*) as a mid or half-open vowel, front or centralised from front (of the [ɛ] or [ë] variety), had already been reached by at least the eighteenth century (the corresponding back vowel was doubtless similarly already [ʌ]). But at some point middle-class Scots have learned to realise this vowel, as in non-Scottish varieties of Standard English, as the closer [ɪ]. It seems quite likely that this too was an achievement of the eighteenth-century accent anglicisers. (But the abandoned native Scots realisation remains as a relic in middle-class Scottish speech as vowel *4a* in Table 5:1, in *ever*, *devil*, *whether*, *together*, *next* and the rest.)[13]

The occurrence in certain syntactic conditions of an epenthetic vowel between certain vowels and a following sonorant consonant (as in *sair* [ˈseːʊr], *sore* [ˈsoːʊr]) or between sonorant consonants (as in *airm* [ˈerʌm] or *arm* [ˈarʌm], producing disyllabic realisations of 'monosyllabic words' (as these are in other accents), is a widespread feature of modern vernacular Scots speech (and similar phenomena can be heard in some American, Canadian and other accents).

There are slight indications in some Older Scots spellings[14] that this is an ancient Scots phenomenon, a supposition that its wide regional prevalence today would support.[15] But it is evidently avoided, admittedly not always with total success, by middle-class Scottish speakers and the social stigma it carries is a frequent subject of overt allusion by them (almost as much as that accorded the 'glottal-stop' feature).[16] We do not know exactly when in the past the Scottish middle classes first learned to eliminate (partially) this tell-tale working-class feature from their habits of speaking, but that it was during the period of accent modification of the eighteenth century is a fair guess.

The accent features so far mentioned are characteristic of nearly all middle-class speakers of Scottish Standard English, including users of Professor Abercrombie's 'Basic Scottish Vowel System' (the *most* fully Scottish he treats: see Chapter 5 pp 73–74), despite the fact that in the respects just discussed the realisations in question represent adjustments *away from* fully native Scots speech in the direction of non-Scottish (in fact, no doubt, middle-class London English) pronunciation.

We have now identified certain pronunciation habits shared by present-day middle-class and working-class Scots speakers as part of their shared native Scottish speech-tradition. And we have also noted features where the one or the other variety has innovated away from the older tradition, the middle-class innovations in an anglicising direction, in the sense that these innovations have brought this variety closer to the middle-class English speech represented today by RP and similar accents. In this way a number of social differentials have been achieved. All of these that we have so far considered have been at the level of accent—of sound-system and sound-realisation.

Scotticisms

Some speakers of Scottish Standard English have other relics of Scottish tradition which have escaped the anglicising net, in specific word-*forms*, like [lɛnθ] and [strɛnθ], as against [lɛŋθ] and [strɛŋθ]—the forms *lenth* and *strenth* were already Scots by the fourteenth century (see *A Dictionary of the Older Scottish Tongue, s.vv*)—and [lʌdʒ] and [ˈlʌdʒɪr], *ludge* and *ludger*, as against [lɔdʒ] and [ˈlɔdʒɪr], *lodge* and *lodger*; the forms *ludge* and *ludger* commemorate a fifteenth-century exclusively Scots sound-change,[17] *thare* [ðeːr] and *whare* [ʍeːr] as against *there* [ðɛːr] and *where* [ʍɛːr], and *fift, sixt* and *nineteent*. Other characteristically Scots forms found commonly in Scottish Standard English speech are ['rasbɛrɪ] not ['razbrɪ] *raspberry*, ['lʌgʒurɪ] not ['lʌkʃurɪ] *luxury*, and the similar things mentioned by Professor Abercrombie in Chapter 5 on p 70–71, *Wednesday* with three, not two, syllables ['wɛdn̩zdɪ] not ['wɛnzdɪ], *tortoise* and *porpoise* with level stress, ['tɔr'tɔɪz], ['pɔr'pɔɪz] not ['tɔːtəs], ['pɔːpəs], and some other escapees of the general anglicising of older French word-stress patterns, like [riʌ'laez] not ['riəlaɪz] *realise*.

Middle-class Scottish Standard English is rather more Scottish in its grammar than has hitherto been realised, though, like everything else in this paper, this is a phenomenon of the spoken not the written language. Witness the following: the Scottish preference for *he's not going, he'll not go, is he not going?* over *he isn't going, he won't go, isn't he going?*; the Scottish eschewing of *may* and *shall*, a less free use of *must* and *ought* and a more restricted set of uses for *should* than in other kinds of English—*can I come in?* not *may I?*; *he'll maybe come later* not *he may*; also *will* or *'ll* replacing the *shall* of other English; and *you'll have to go* favoured over *you must go, you should get up earlier* favoured over *ought to*, and *I would, if I was you* not *I should, if I were you. Need, use to* and *dare* are constructed as lexical verbs not as modals—so *do you dare to do it?* not *dare you do it?*—; but *need* and *want* and some other verbs of related meaning have distinctively Scottish constructions—*the car needs/wants washed, the cat needs/wants out*. Still other features include: the favouring of progressive forms for these and other verbs, such as *hope*—*I am hoping to be present*—; 'double auxiliary' constructions of *can* and *could*—*they'll can see to it* or *I'd could have done it*—; *I'll better* for *I'd better*; quasi-elliptical constructions such as *that's me away home* or *I'll away out*; the tendency to avoid *wh*-forms of the relative in favour of *that*,—giving *the folk that fell* rather than *the men who fell*, or *the people that's houses were demolished* (or *that the houses were demolished of*) rather than *whose*, or *our Bill that's always complaining* rather than *who's*. Finally, there is the absolute possessive *mines*.

The following more or less exclusively Scottish idioms, clichés and single words come far short of exhausting the list of such items in regular and more or less unselfconscious use by most middle-class speakers of Scottish Standard English: I *doubt* he's not coming; I *doubt* he's got lost; what would you like for *your* Christmas; I'm away to *my* bed; to take *the* flu, go to *the* church or *the* school; *and him* an elder of the kirk too; *and you* pregnant; a week *on* Sunday; to be up *through* the night; are you *never* out your bed yet?; you're *never* going out in that state!; how's he *keeping*? He's *keeping* fine; to *stay* in a (*housing-*) *scheme* (= local authority housing estate); to *shed* (= part) one's hair; *to miss oneself*; the whole *jingbang* or *bangshoot* (= caboodle); *I put her gas at a peep* (= I quashed her); *to give someone a row* /rʌu/ (= a scolding); *I can see Christmas far enough* (= I've had enough of it); *I could see him far enough*; the walls were *living* (= alive) with bugs; he has a good *conceit* of himself; *if it comes up my back* (=comes to hand, occurs to me to undertake something); I'll see you *the length of* (= as far as) the bus-stop; *the back of* (= not long after) nine; *don't let on* (= reveal by your actions) you've seen him; and *bramble, burn* (brook), *rone-pipe* (drainpipe), *haar* (thick sea mist), *rowan* (mountain ash), *pinkie* (little finger), *ashet* (large serving-plate), *to jag* (prick), *to sort* (mend), *to swither* (hesitate), and the exclamations *ach!* *och!* and (in the precise Scottish realisation of this) *mphm* ['m:m̥m̩ʔ].

These are examples of what we may call covert (or 'unmarked') Scotticisms; that is, more or less exclusively Scottish usages employed by many Scottish speakers without their being very much or at all aware that in so doing they are revealing their Scottish origins, that these *are* peculiarly Scottish usages. Some are recent innovations—*to put somebody's gas at a peep*, obviously, or *to miss oneself*, apparently (the latter first recorded in *The Scottish National Dictionary* for the 1960s). Others, like most of the characteristics of pronunciation specified above, return to medieval or early modern Scots: including the avoidance of *wh-* relatives, the ellipsis in *I'll away out* (albeit this is also in earlier southern English, where, however, it is now obsolete), the form *mines*, *to let on* (originally *to let on oneself*), and *the length of* (the last three all from the seventeenth century) and all of the one-word items listed. Like the accent features already discussed, these ancient covert Scotticisms similarly commemorate the native Scots affiliations of the Scottish Standard English of middle-class Scots speakers.

The other kinds of Scotticism which mark modern

'educated' or middle-class Scottish speech are almost by definition of a highly traditional Scottish character, and almost all of them have characterised Scottish speech and to a great extent Scots vernacular writing since the Middle Ages. These are cultural Scotticisms—those which refer to peculiarly Scottish aspects of life in Scotland and so naturally possess native Scots labels, like *laird* or *kirk-session* or *first-foot* or *ceilidh*—and overt (or 'marked') Scotticisms. The latter is the designation I am accustomed to give to that special diction of Scottish-tagged locutions used self-consciously by many Scottish speakers as a kind of stylistic grace and as a way of claiming membership of the in-group of Scotsmen. For this purpose any traditional Scots word or expression will serve, like *aye* for *yes*, *dinna* for *don't*, and *hame* and *hoose* and *ben the hoose* and *bairns* (children) and *birl* (to spin) and *coup* (to capsize) and *ken* (to know) and *stot* (to bounce) and *gey* (very) and many other comparatively commonplace native Scots words (in short, material from column 1 of Table 6:1). As well as, on occasion, rarer, more exotic and more localised items, the latter presenting themselves especially when a Scot from a provincial (non-Edinburgh) region of Scotland encounters a fellow provincial outwith the native province: one thinks, for example, of the expatriate Aberdonian's ritual greeting of a fellow expatriate from the same region, 'Foo are ye the day, man?' and its equally ritual reply, 'Och, jist chaavin.'

There also exists a limited number (several hundred?) of these expressions which seem specially favoured by middle-class English-speaking Scots, so as to constitute a highly recurrent set of stereotypes: Is he still *to the fore* (alive)? He's a right old *sweetiewife* (literally, woman who sells sweetmeats, i.e. gossip, chatterbox), or, a bit of a *feardie* (a coward), *a drop o the auld kirk* or *o the craitur* (a small amount of whisky), *that'll not set the heather on fire* (cause any stir), *let that flee stick to the wa* (say no more about that matter), *it's back to the auld claes and parritch* (to humdrum everyday life) *tomorrow*, *come into the body of the kirk* (come and join the main company—said e.g. to one sitting apart), *to keep a calm sough* (to keep quiet or not to get excited), and *slàinte-mhath* (Gaelic for 'Good health!'); and certain *couthy* (homely) Scots words like *clamjamfry* (a confused mixture) and *chuckiestanes* (pebbles) and *darg* (a job of work) and a *dram* (a drink of whisky) and *orra* (odd) and *thrang* (busy, engrossed) and *dreich* (dry, tedious) and *wersh* (bitter or insipid) and *stravaig* (to wander aimlessly) and *peelie-wallie* (somewhat ill, sickly) and *wabbit* (exhausted) and *shoogly* (shaky, unsteady).

These stereotyped 'marked Scotticisms' and some traditional Scots 'dialect' words feature as occasional embellishments of middle-class Scottish Standard English speech on appropriate informal and formal occasions (for example, in speechmaking to provide a more or less jocular reminder that the speaker is a good Scot). Knowledge of some of these items is reinforced by reading in the vernacular Scots classics (such as the novels of Scott). Accordingly, some, at any rate, appear to be employed more often by 'educated' Scots speakers than by their less erudite working-class fellow-countrymen, and appear almost to constitute a kind of middle-class folklore of what identifies the true Scot in speech.

Perhaps most of the list of overt Scotticisms just given belong specially to these middle-class speakers of Scottish Standard English.

Some native and exclusively Scottish words and expressions are thus shared by middle-class speakers of 'Scottish Standard English' and working-class speakers of 'Scots' (that is, of speech-styles drawing more copiously and unselfconsciously on material from columns 1 and 2 of Table 6:1). There are other expressions of a 'covert Scotticism' variety which are of more doubtful, or less assured, or less general, middle-class acceptability.

How widely current are *what a laugh if* (something were so) or *what a pant if* (compare *what a joke if*)? Or compare *that's a laugh* with *that's a joke*. Is *to phone up* as widely acceptable as *to phone* or *to ring up*? (Not long ago it apparently was not; now one also hears the Americanism *to call*.) How does *to go the messages* (go shopping) compare for acceptability with *go for the messages*? to take something *off of the top* with *off the top*? Some but perhaps not all middle-class Scots would find acceptable *to go one's dinger* (to act in a very energetic or extravagant way) or *to be up to high doh* (greatly perturbed) *about something*, or the adjective *puggled* or *pugglet* ['pʌgl̩t] (exhausted), the verbs *to humph* (to 'hump', carry laboriously) and *to chum* (to accompany), the idiom *that's me* or *that's him* etc (doing or having to do something), as in *that's me humphing*, or *having*

to humph, it away out to Blackhall or *having to chum
her right down to the station*; the exclamation *here!* (= see!
look!)—*and here! the shop was open after all*—and the interrogative tag *ai*, realised as [e] or [ɪʔ] (? a reduction of *in't it?*,
i.e. [ɪn ʔɪʔ]) as *you'll be wantin your tea, ai?* (with falling
intonation). Of course, there are similar variations in acceptability of colloquialisms which are not confined to Scotland, like *to be able to go* (something to eat, as *I could fair go
a pie*), which appears to have a narrower range of social
acceptability than *to feel like* (something to eat, as *I feel like a
pie*); but in Scotland many of the items which vary in social
acceptability in this way are indeed more or less exclusive to
Scottish speech.

Moving still further down the scale of acceptability to
middle-class Scottish Standard English speakers, there are a
number of well-known shibboleths of Central Scots urban
working-class speech, apparently mostly of comparatively
recent origin (that is, they are at once restricted in their
social, regional and chronological distribution), which seldom
or never occur, except by way of mockery of other speakers,
in middle-class Scottish speech. Such 'vulgarisms' include the
intensifier *awfie*, the disparaging term *teenie-bash* (for a
woman whom one dislikes), the expression *to loss the heid* (=
to lose one's senses, run amock), the asseverative tag *ken*, as
in *Weel—ken—ye dinny pey—ken—for i'[ʔɪ] jist watch—
ken* (the unreduced *ye ken* seems to carry less stigma), the
interrogative tag *ai-no* [eˑno]—*You'll be wantin your tea,
ai-no?*, and in west central Scotland, the attention-focussing
idiom with imperative *See* as in *See our Mary, she's awfie
shy*, and the asseverative tag *so he, it* etc *is, was, does* etc, as
he's awfie tired, so he is; as well as such stock music-hall
stereotypes as the exclamations *crivvens! jings! help ma bob!*
Similarly stigmatised working-class grammatical features,
some occurring also in non-standard English furth of Scotland, include the rather new plural-marked pronoun *youse*
(for *you*) or *youse-yins*, the use of *us*, or *'s*, with singular
reference (*give us it* or *gie's it* or *see's it*), the sentence-final
adverbial tag use of *but* (*you meant it, but*) (the similar use of
though—*you meant it, though*—is more generally acceptable), the tag *an' that* (= standard *and so on*), multiple
negation, as *I never saw none*, the well-known syncretisms of
past tense and past participle forms as in *I never seen him*, or
ye'd have saw him if ye'd a came, (and cf p 98), and the usage

with the reduced form of infinitive *have* (as *a* [ʌ]) after *had*, as in the conditional clause of the following example: *If ye had a said, we wid a kent and we could a went.*

These are items which do not normally accompany the middle-class accent and other usages described above. *Their* normal company is working-class accent features (cf p 102f) and a freer and less stereotyped recourse to columns 1 and 2 in Table 6:1 than middle-class Scots speakers commonly permit themselves.

In truth we are totally lacking in any but impressionistic observations of the frequency, occasions of incidence, and distributions by region, socio-economic class, sex, age and degree of style formality, of all of these different categories of Scotticisms. But it is at least evident that there are a number of different sets each with its own range of stylistic appropriateness and social acceptability.

Other Accents: 'Anglo-English' and 'hybrid'
In ranging between 'middle-class' and 'working-class' Scottish speech as we have just done we have not of course covered the entire spectrum of the socially delimited varieties of English speech in Scotland. One variety not yet mentioned is that which is the more or less exclusive property of the Scottish laird class, the county gentlefolk of Scotland, and some other members of middle- or upper-class Scottish society (also including, of course, some immigrants from England). The sharing by such people of the accent of English which characterises the ruling classes of England (Received Pronunciation or RP, see p 73) follows from the fact that the Scottish and English aristocracies have been closely intermingled since the seventeenth century, partly by intermarriage and partly by their sharing the same education—in English boarding-schools and Oxbridge (see p 92).

Though the feelings of many Scots about the kind of English which characterises such speakers seem ambivalent—it simultaneously raises hackles and overawes—it is associated with people who are almost universally of high social standing. So it seems possible or even likely that it is imitation by individual speakers with native Scottish accents of the accent of these prestigious speakers that has brought into existence those vowel systems of Scottish Standard English which may be regarded as hybrids between the most fully Scottish system described by Professor Abercrombie in

Chapter 5 (his 'Basic System') and the system which these prestigious speakers themselves use—namely, RP (or Professor Abercrombie's 'Anglo-English' system). And it also seems likely that a continuing influence of this sort at the present day helps to maintain these hybrid systems or perhaps even encourage their wider adoption. These are systems which on p 75ff Professor Abercrombie described as modifications of the Basic System towards the Anglo-English System, at the same time stressing that they are fully established and institutionalised.

Systemic modifications are not the only modifications in an Anglo-English direction which Scottish speakers of Standard English display. The accents of all middle-class Scottish speakers of Standard English, whether users of the Basic System or of one of the Modified Basic systems, also display the results of certain adjustments of distribution and realisation, likewise long-established and institutionalised, away from older traditional pronunciation habits and towards Anglo-English. Some of these were instanced on pp 102–103 above, as resulting, certainly or probably, from eighteenth-century anglicisations of the middle-class Scottish accent—the /ɔ/ and /o/ (vowel *8*/vowel *9*) re-distribution, the 'educated' realisation of the /ɪ/ phoneme as a closer vowel [ɪ] than the vernacular [ɛ] or [ë], and the partial elimination of the pronunciation with epenthetic vowel of such words as *sore* and *arm*. Indeed the possession of these particular anglicised features and some others is all but criterial for the 'educated' or socially 'acceptable' middle-class accents of Scottish English.

There also exist accents of middle-class Scottish speech which, in addition to the distributional and realisational characteristics just mentioned, also display others which look very much like the results of further adjustments away from traditional Scots pronunciation habits in the direction of RP (or 'Anglo-English'). One of these is described in Chapter 5, p 80, by Professor Abercrombie: the reduction of the 'fully Scottish' sub-system of four vowels, *2, 4a, 4* and *12*, /ɪ/, /ë/, /ɛ/ and /ʌ/, before /r/ (as in [bɪrθ], [ërθ], [pɛrθ], and [wʌrθ]) to a single central vowel, frequently accompanied however by realisation of /r/ either as frictionless continuant or as 'r-colouring'. Another which Professor Abercrombie mentions (p 81) is the diphthongal realisations of vowels *3* (as [ei]) and *9* (as [oɑ]). Other features which, like these, seem usually or always to accompany one of Professor Abercrombie's Modified Basic systems rather than his Basic System, include the sporadic or consistent failure to realise /r/ pre-consonantally, e.g. in *farm* [faːm] or *form* [fɔːm] or even finally, e.g. in *far* [faː] or *before* [biˈfɔː], apparently irrespective of the preceding vowel, and a sporadic or, for some speakers, consistent merging of vowels *13* and *14* (under [aʊ]). Detailed and systematic observations of these phenomena remain to be carried out, but on my own casual observation I have no doubt of their existence among some members of the Scottish middle classes, including some well-known Scottish broadcasters, such as Douglas Kynoch and Harry Gray, though I do not know how far their spread correlates with, for example, speakers' region, age and sex. Nor do I know whether they fit, along with Professor Abercrombie's 'modifications' to the Basic System, into a larger hierarchical arrangement than he described, or one more randomly arranged.

The features mentioned in the last but one paragraph are present in the speech of virtually all middle-class though not all working-class Scots and of most Scots who have received a higher education. I have therefore suggested that we may regard these features as *criterial* for 'educated' or middle-class Scottish Standard English speech. On the other hand, the features described in the last paragraph, while it is my impression that they are largely (or entirely) confined to middle-class speakers, are not in the same way found in anything like *all* speakers who might claim middle-class membership, and so may be looked upon as merely *optional* features for this class of speakers. But they certainly do occur in *many* such speakers; it may even turn out that the majority of the present-day Scottish establishment have in their speech one or more features of this set.

If we assume that these optional middle-class Scottish Standard English accent features are likely to be of more recent origin than the criterial ones mentioned above, then we have to suppose them to have been established as late as the nineteenth or even the present century; in fact, before the last few years, I am aware of explicit mention of only one of them (the reduction of /ɪr/, /ër/, /ɛr/ and /ʌr/), in 1913.[18] Accents containing one or more of these optional features more closely approximate to an Anglo-English or RP accent than do accents which contain only the criterial middle-class Scottish Standard English features. The widespread existence of such accents, and of accents having one of Professor Abercrombie's first three Modified Basic systems, thus apparently manifests a still further shift in an anglicising direction of the centre of gravity or norm of 'educated' or middle-class Scottish speech. As their widespread middle-class occurrence would suggest, 'hybrid' accents of this kind seem to attract little popular attention and receive little or no adverse middle-class comment: they are just as acceptable as, or perhaps more acceptable than, accents which employ the Basic System and possess *only* those features which are criterial for 'educated' Scottish Standard English speech.

This is not the case, however, with the so-called 'Kelvinside' or 'Morningside' accents which for some time have been widely disapproved as supposedly indicating pretentiousness or affectation. Though some use these labels less precisely and specifically, for many Scots they appear to designate those accents of Scottish Standard English in which regular middle-class or lower middle-class Scots features are accompanied, perhaps only sporadically, by a few specific, seemingly 'hyper-correct' realisational features, namely the vowel-qualities roughly indicated in such spellings as *ectually*, *Egnes*—[ε] in place of more usual [a]; *naise* (= nice) and *faine* (= fine)—[ei] in place of more usual [əi] or [ʌi]; often along with special features of vowel-length, rhythm and voice-quality. These certainly appear to be the result of inaccurate, 'overshooting' or 'over-compensating' attempts to adjust the native realisations of these sounds to the more prestigious RP pronunciations.

It seems unfair that these particular adjustments should be specially singled out for stigmatisation since, as we have just seen, all the widely approved 'educated' Scottish accents of Standard English display the results of some assimilations, both in system and in realisations, to southern English pronunciation. Maybe the difference is that these last are less noticeably inaccurate. And perhaps they are longer established.

The labels 'Kelvinside' and 'Morningside' as designating some such accent stereotype have been in use only since about the turn of the present century (see p 98, and *svv* in *The Scottish National Dictionary*), and there appear to be no indications of the earlier existence of precisely this variety, either as reality or as stereotype. How widely accents containing these features are distributed is at present unknown,

but they do not seem to be confined to the districts designated
in their popular names and they are certainly far from universal or even common there. But they are not mythical:
speakers presenting these features do exist, and their speech
can be identified with the stereotype and does evoke un-
favourable comment from other speakers.

If it is true that the Modified Basic vowel systems and
'hybrid' middle-class accents of the sort described above are
becoming more common, and hence, presumably, that the
norm or centre of gravity of educated Scottish speech is
becoming progressively less fully Scots, should this cause us
concern? Setting aside nostalgic regrets for such things as
alleged loss of national identity, renunciation of a people's
'roots' and the like, it might be argued also that such trends
could have the effect of impeding social mobility, which
some, this writer included, might regard as unfortunate.

We might argue in this way. A former norm of middle-
class Scottish speech may have been an accent with Professor Abercrombie's 'Basic Scottish Vowel System' and with
the criterial but without the optional distributional and realisational characteristics. As we have seen (pp 102–104), this
differs in several respects from working-class Scottish
speech: for example, in operating a much lower frequency of
glottal stop substitutions for *t*, in having closer realisations
of /ɪ/, in having a different distribution of the /o/ and /ɔ/
phonemes, with a higher incidence of /ɔ/, and so on. So
socially mobile people with native working-class accents had
all this to assimilate if they were to move into the charmed
circle of speakers with 'educated' accents. But the new, still
more anglicised, 'hybrid' accents are at a still farther remove
from working-class vernacular speech. If these become the
norm of 'polite' Scottish speech, socially mobile, originally
working-class speakers will now have to learn not only
everything they had to learn before, but in addition such
things as: a reduction of the four- or three-way distinction of
/ɪr/, /ër/, /ɛr/ and /ʌr/ to one item, to replace by one of the
'weaker' realisations or entirely eliminate their trilled or flap-
ped [r] before consonants and word-finally, to diphthongise
certain hitherto monophthongal vowel realisations (namely /e/
and /o/) and to introduce some of the new vowel distinctions
of Professor Abercrombie's Modified Basic systems. Thus
their task, which is not only to make these adjustments but to
do so accurately, so that they do not betray by inaccurate

performance the fact that they *are* engaged in social climbing in this respect, is made that much harder. May not this extra linguistic distance which we are now asking people to jump mean that some who would otherwise have made it must now fall short of the promised land of full social acceptability of their speech?

Accent Tolerance

All this presupposes of course that accent *is* important to one's admissibility in middle-class society, and to the self-confidence and ease with which one moves within it. In an ideal world, accent would not of course matter. People would concern themselves about what other people said and not about the accent in which they said it. Happily we are perhaps closer to that ideal than we were thirty years ago. Among the young people I meet around Edinburgh University there seem to be more who appear unconcerned about their own or others' accents than in my own generation. But it would also be idle to pretend that most people do not evaluate others socially on the basis of their accent (among other things), and that for certain kinds of career and certain sorts of social success, to possess an 'educated' accent is at least advantageous and perhaps even indispensable.

If we accept this argument, that the further anglicisation of the norm of educated Scottish speech is undesirable for this reason, what can we do about it? Should we be self-consciously working at Scotticising and vernacularising our own accents, so moving, hopefully with other people doing the same, in a direction contrary to the trend which we deplore? One drawback—no doubt among others—to this suggestion is the adverse effect which the constant monitoring of our speech-performance that this would entail might have on our fluency. And there is the risk, if too few of us attempt this, of our simply becoming linguistic eccentrics. Perhaps a more generally effective step might be that of urging more strenuously that the authorities who manage the broadcasting media display more favour to the more Scots and vernacular kinds of accent than they at present do. Another rather differently-directed move towards the same ultimate objective would be to support the campaign for 'accent tolerance' on which some linguists are already engaged: in itself this does not call for the favouring of *any* accent, whether more or less Scots, so this at least, if successful, would mean that an attempt to 'save' the more Scots accents would be beside the point. This would seem to tie in best with the trend toward greater unconcern about accent which, as I suggested above, may be happening among younger people in a socially freer and less class-conscious society than we have had in the past.

In any case, the picture is not by any means wholly black. Despite all the anglicisation of Scottish speech which has gone on through recent centuries, there is still, as the above pages and the rest of this book have shown, a vast amount of Scots material current in everyday spoken usage, of both middle-class and working-class Scottish speakers, as well as in our literary and oral traditions generally. Accents of 'educated' Scottish Standard English which retain many Scots features shared with working-class Scottish speech and continuing centuries-old native speech habits are still tolerated in most spheres of Scottish society.

1 The phenomenon of a bipolar continuum in speech, particularly Scottish speech, is discussed at greater length and in more general terms by Tom McArthur in the first section of Chapter 4 of this book. A perceptive earlier discussion, also with reference to Scottish speech, appeared in Trevor Hill, 'Institutional linguistics' *Orbis* 7, 1958, p 450, in advance of Ferguson's (1959) discussion of 'diglossia': see note 3 to Chapter 4. I have also some further discussion of the Scottish situation in 'The Scots language and the teacher of English in Scotland', in *Scottish Literature in the Secondary School* (Edinburgh: Scottish Education Department, 1976) pp 48–55.

2 Rosalind K Marshall, *The House of Hamilton in its Anglo-Scottish Setting in the Seventeenth Century* (Ph D thesis, University of Edinburgh, 1970) pp 44–49; 108–109.

3 See L E C MacQueen, *The Last Stages of the Older Literary Language of Scotland* (PhD Thesis, University of Edinburgh, 1957) pp 179–180; 249–250; 275–276; 446ff.

4 See G Donaldson, 'Foundations of Anglo-Scottish Union' in S T Bindoff (ed), *Elizabethan Government and Society: Essays Presented to Sir John Neale* (London: Athlone Press, 1961) pp 296–299; and MacQueen, *op cit* p 250.

5 See his Preface to *The Ever Green* (1724) in *The Works of Allan Ramsay*, Scottish Text Society 4 Ser, 6, 1970, p 237, where he castigates the 'affected Class of Fops' who, shown 'the most elegant Thoughts in a Scots Dress, they did as disdainfully as stupidly condemn it as barbarous'.

6 See 'Invocation' to his *Helenore or the Fortunate Shepherdess*

(1768) in *The Scottish Works of Alexander Ross, M A*, Scottish Text Society 3 Ser, 9, 1935 (1938), p 11:

> Speak my ain leed, 'tis gueed auld Scots I mean;
> Your Southren gnaps I count not worth a preen.
> We've words a fouth, that we can ca' our ain,
> Tho' frae them now my childer sair refrain,
> An' are to my gueed auld proverb confeerin,
> Neither gueed fish nor flesh, nor yet sa't herrin.

7 These matters have been written up many times, for example by MacQueen, *op cit* (note 3), especially chapters 1, 7 and 8; David Craig, *Scottish Literature and the Scottish People 1680–1830* (London: Chatto & Windus, 1961), especially chapters 2 and 8 and notes thereto; J A Smith, 'Some eighteenth century ideas of Scotland' in N T Phillipson & R Mitchison (eds), *Scotland in the Age of Improvement* (Edinburgh University Press, 1970) pp 107ff; and Janet M Templeton, 'Scots: an outline history' in A J Aitken (ed), *Lowland Scots* (Association for Scottish Literary Studies Occasional Papers No 2, Edinburgh, 1973) pp 8–10. The ludicrous aspects of the vogue when at its height around 1760 have been entertainingly recalled by Robert McLellan in his play *The Flouers o Edinburgh* (1947).

8 For eighteenth-century examples see Craig, *op cit* pp 318–319.

9 The Rule has been mentioned many times under various names since J A H Murray first described it, perceptively and quite comprehensively, in his *The Dialect of the Southern Counties of Scotland* (London, 1873) pp 97–98. The fullest account to date is that of Paul Wettstein, *The Phonology of a Berwickshire Dialect* (Switzerland, 1942) pp 6–11. Recent mentions include that by R Lass in his 'Linguistic orthogenesis? Scots vowel quantity and the English length conspiracy' in J M Anderson & C Jones (eds), *Historical Linguistics* (Amsterdam: North-Holland Publishing Company, 1974) 2, pp 311–343; by Mary V Taylor in 'The great Southern Scots conspiracy: pattern in the development of Northern English' *ibid*, pp 403–406; by A J Aitken in 'How to pronounce Older Scots' in A J Aitken, Matthew P MacDiarmid & Derick S Thomson (eds) *Bards and Makars: Scottish Language and Literature, Medieval and Renaissance* (Glasgow University Press, 1977) pp 8–9, and also in *The Scottish Vowel-length Rule* (duplicated).

10 More properly, /jeːz/, /meːr/ and /jɪs/, /gɪd/, since what we have here is the 'split' of an originally single phoneme, and the re-allocation of its word-group, as predicted by the Rule, to two other phonemes: those words for which the Rule predicts the 'long' realisation joining the vowel of *raise* /reːz/ and *mare* /meːr/ (more), and words with the 'short' realisation the vowel of *miss*, /mɪs/ and *lid*, /lɪd/.

11 For an eighteenth-century anecdote on this subject, see K Kohler, 'A late eighteenth-century comparison of the "Provincial Dialect of Scotland" and the "Pure Dialect"' *Linguistics* **23**, 1966, p 52 (and on the whole question of /ɔ/ and /o/, *ibid* pp 50–54). Compare also James Elphinston, *Propriety Ascertained in her Picture* (London, 1787) 1, p 265: '*Pollish and Polish, modest and modish, morral and oral, primmer and primer* ... will no more claim respectively won strong vowel.'

12 See e.g. Kohler, *op cit* p 54 (also p 44), and the various modern accounts of this dialect.

13 See Kohler, *op cit* pp 48–49, also M L Samuels, *Linguistic Evolution* (Cambridge University Press 1972) pp 98–99.

14 These spelling data are of course accessible in the *Dictionary of the Older Scottish Tongue* (*DOST*), entries for the various words potentially displaying this feature.

15 See e.g. J A H Murray, *op cit* (note 9) p 125; E Dieth, *A Grammar of the Buchan Dialect* (Cambridge University Press, 1932), pp 70–72; 96–97; P Wettstein, *op cit* (note 9) p 16; R Zai, *The Phonology of the Morebattle District* (Switzerland, 1942) p 141 (§229). This feature, which appears to occur most regularly at the tone-group nucleus, is not realised in certain other morphological and syntactic conditions: see the Dieth references for examples of some of these and contrast [ɩ ˈhʌd ʌ ˈseːr ˈeˑrʌm] *he had a sair airum*, and [ɩz ˈerm̩z n̩ ˈlɛgz wɩz ˈɔfɩ ˈseːɩr] *his airms an legs wis awfy sai-er*.

16 But those 'educated' Scots speakers who remain fully rhotic (see p 69) regularly have disyllabic pronunciations of what are in other accents monosyllabic words like *arm* and *barn*, realising the final sonorant consonants as syllabic consonants, i.e. as [arm̩] and [ˈbarn̩] (which in this accent is homophonous with *barren*, also [ˈbarn̩]) and *burn* [ˈbʌrn̩]. However, while [ˈarm̩] is 'acceptable', [ˈarʌm] is not: thus in his *The Pronunciation of English in Scotland* (Cambridge University Press, 1913) pp 55–56, and also in *Speech Training for Scottish Students* (Cambridge University Press, 1925) p 97, William Grant deprecates the latter type of pronunciation as 'very objectionable' while accepting or recommending the former.

17 Whereby /o/ merged with /u/ (of which the modern reflex is /ʌ/) before /tʃ/ or /dʒ/: see **Luge** n. in *DOST* (etym. note) and also **Bruche, Cruchet,** and Older Scots **sudgeorn** (= sojourn).

18 W Grant, *The Pronunciation of English* p 62, but more explicitly *Speech Training* pp 105–106. In Anne H McAllister, *A Year's Course in Speech Training* (University of London Press, 1963) p 177, the acquisition of [ɜɹ] as a substitute for all of /ɩr/, /ɛr/ and /ʌr/ is held to be specially desirable for 'those Scots who are concerned with acquiring a good Scottish pronunciation free from the more marked provincialisms'.

PART THREE
THE STUDY OF
SCOTLAND'S LANGUAGES

*Papers on the current study of and investigations into Gaelic,
Scots and Scottish Standard English.*

7

The State of
Gaelic Language Studies

Donald MacAulay

What I propose to do in the following article is to take a look at the state of contemporary Scottish Gaelic linguistic research, with brief glances at the basis laid in the past and the potentialities of the future. It will not be possible to discuss everything that is being done; this is especially true of those activities, such as textual studies for example, that have indirect linguistic significance, and research work that is not yet sufficiently developed for its implications to be clear. Such work will at best be mentioned in passing. The following will be incomplete also, no doubt, in that there may be research in progress that I have not heard about. For such shortcomings I should like to apologise in advance—even to those who did not answer my requests for information! To those who kindly responded to my requests I should like to express my grateful thanks.

There are at present only two major funded linguistic projects concerned with Scottish Gaelic. These are the historical dictionary being prepared in Glasgow University (to which we will return later) and the Gaelic section of the Linguistic Survey of Scotland.

The Gaelic Survey, established nearly thirty years ago in the University of Edinburgh, is concerned with gathering and processing data to establish the differential distribution of forms over the Gaelic-speaking area of Scotland. Its final product is envisaged as a dialect atlas defining areas of linguistic similarity and their boundaries. This is a task of some magnitude, and that, as well as the limited nature of its funds, no doubt explains the time that it has taken to come to fruition. The present situation is that the major task of data-gathering has been completed and a secondary round of mini-surveys, evolved from the initial data and designed to supplement it, is in process. One hopes to see published results in the not too distant future. Until this comes about, we are dependent for our dialect information on the survey of

Scottish material presented in Volume IV of the *Irish Lin-guistic Atlas* (Wagner & Ó Baoill 1969, Appendix I); on Borgstrøm's dialect surveys in the Outer Hebrides, Skye and Ross-shire (Borgstrøm 1940; 1941) and on monograph studies of individual dialects. Fortunately there are a fair number of these, ranging from Gunn 1889, MacBain 1892, and Robertson 1906–1909 (itself a mini-survey), to Holmer 1938 (and later 1957 and 1962), Borgstrøm 1937, Oftedal 1956, Watson 1974 and Dorian 1978. These monographs are supplemented by reference in studies of particular themes which utilise material from different sources (notably Ternes 1973; see also Ó Murchú 1976 and MacGill-Fhinnein 1966), so that the information available to us is considerable. Work of this kind is continuing to be done by different individuals. For exam-ple, Hank Rogers is preparing a study of the Gaelic of Eriskay and James Gleasure, of Glasgow University, is working on Ardnamurchan Gaelic. Nevertheless there are still gaps in the data (some, indeed, which we can no longer fill), the material is in some cases of doubtful value, and some of it is much overtaken by time. Many of these shortcomings will, it is hoped, be remedied by the Linguistic Survey. Its coverage and precision should provide us with a definitive statement of dialect distribution and even enable us, in some instances at least, to compare the situation as it stands now with that obtaining twenty-five years ago.

One of the problems with surveys, of course, has been that they have been regarded as the answer to all problems of linguistic research, whereas in fact they usually deal with fairly narrow linguistic areas, often from a particular point of view, leaving many other areas untouched. For Gaelic, we especially need a programme of syntactic research to com-plement the work done in the Survey. We also need to plan for what is to follow the work of the Survey in other areas.

The Sound System
The Survey concentrates on the Gaelic sound system (and on the morphological system) and in this it follows precedent. Indeed, from the earliest studies we have mentioned, such as Robertson for example, through the works of Borgstrøm and Oftedal to the most recent work of Watson and Dorian, the emphasis has been in the first instance on the sound system.

The approaches to the sound system have varied, however. We have a development from unsystematic to sys-

tematic phonetics—comparing Robertson with Wagner & Ó
Baoill, and Borgstrøm. From there we move to taxonomic
phonemics with Oftedal 1956 and Dorian 1978, and especially
with Ternes 1973, whose strict and uncompromising phonemic interpretations seem to me to push a strong version of
that theory to the crucial point of testability with relation to
Scottish Gaelic for, perhaps, the first time.

Certain aspects of the sound system have proved more
interesting to linguists than others, and it is in connection
with these in particular that other theoretical viewpoints have
been brought to bear on the language. This has, perhaps
inevitably considering its complexity, been the case with
morphophonology, especially features of initial mutation,
which have fascinated linguists since Bonaparte (1882). These
have been dealt with by Oftedal, Ternes and Dorian from a
phonemic point of view (see also Hamp 1951, Oftedal 1962a,
for example, for a wider Celtic analysis from this point of
view). An interesting recent analysis is Ó Murchú 1976. This
study of the article + noun structure in Perthshire demonstrates a state of the language where mutation distinctively
signals the presence of the article over a much wider area
than is usually the case—or, to be more precise, signals the
presence of those systems usually associated with an overt
article (cf Dorian 1978).

I have looked at the problem from a (modified) prosodic
analysis standpoint (MacAulay 1962; see Oftedal 1963 for a
phonemically based objection to part of this, and my reply:
MacAulay 1966; see also Ellis 1965). Rogers (1972) has looked
at the matter from the viewpoint of generative phonology, as
has Cram 1975. In spite of the attention the problem has
received, it cannot be said that there is much agreement about
solutions, but the area remains a popular one for trying out
linguistic theories. Recently my colleague in Aberdeen,
Cathair Ó Dochartaigh, and I myself, have been taking a new
look at some aspects in terms of 'dependency phonology'.
This promises to be of considerable interest (cf Ó Dochartaigh Forthcoming).

At the phonetic end of the sound system there has been a
good deal less activity. Phonetic analysis is of course a
necessary basis for any serious phonological study, but there
has not been a great deal of research effort put into detailed
phonetic work for its own sake, or into theoretical phonetics,
and this, I think, might sometimes adversely affect phono-

logical conclusions. There has been considerable discussion of such problems as the palatalisation of labials in Gaelic, in, for example, MacAulay 1962 and 1966, Oftedal 1963 and Jackson 1967. It is often maintained that Gaelic labials are not palatalised, but this is certainly not the case *phonetically* in south-west Lewis, though there are clear indications that palatalisation is less stable in labial environments. The problem would become much clearer if we had detailed extensive phonetic data. In fact it has been tackled essentially as a problem of phonological distinctiveness, and as Ternes says (1973, 32) it has not been entirely solved in those terms, a statement which I think still holds despite his own analysis of the Applecross material and his exposition of the different positions taken on the matter.

This neglect of phonetic research applies particularly to acoustic and instrumental investigation. Some work has, of course, been done, mostly in the Department of Linguistics in Edinburgh University. Fred MacAulay produced some palatograms in the early 1950s; Cathair Ó Dochartaigh prepared some kymograms on preaspiration for his Phonetic Diploma thesis in 1967 and has made an additional set more recently in 1977. Cynthia Shuken is making instrumental measurements of various features of the Gaelic sound system as part of her PhD thesis (cf, for example, Shuken 1977).

What we have said about segmental features could be applied with added force to 'suprasegmental' features. General statements on the distribution of stress occur in the more recent dialect monographs and they are by and large accurate. The same cannot always be said of statements on intonation, which are never adequate, and are often misleading. The distribution of pitch in Gaelic is a complicated matter, especially in those dialects which have word tones (see, for example, Oftedal 1956, 26–29); but these word tones are virtually the only pitch feature to have been investigated. I gave a paper on intonation to the Celtic Phonology Congress in Coleraine in 1977 (MacAulay 1979) and another, more recently, to the Aberdeen Linguistics Seminar (MacAulay Forthcoming a), but this only represents a beginning in an area which requires a great deal of detailed study.

Morphology
Gaelic morphology has received considerable attention over the whole range of time in which the language has been

studied, from Shaw 1778 through for example Stewart 1801 to Calder 1923, which is probably the most recent of the traditional studies, and again in the individual monographs mentioned above. These studies take, quite properly, the classical paradigms as their starting point. Traditional treatments generally simply state these, with whatever biases the writer holds (and this is generally true also of the normative statements in pedagogic grammars—cf also Carmody 1945). The dialect monographs generally fit the linguistic forms of the dialects being investigated into the traditional framework for comparison purposes—to measure the degree of deviation from classic norms, for example. It is quite clear from the information to be gathered from the more recent of these publications, for example Dorian 1978 and the forms cited by Watson 1974 and Ó Murchú 1976, and in Wagner & Ó Baoill, that the noun-phrase morphology of Gaelic especially is undergoing very considerable changes and that, indeed, these changes are taking different directions. This is what one might perhaps expect, in the absence of general Gaelic literacy to apply normative pressures, and considering the isolation of mainland Gaelic communities especially, as islands in an English-speaking ocean. The impressions given by these works are certainly borne out in work I have been doing on the morphology of my own dialect (see MacAulay 1978 for some reference to this), and from discussion with colleagues—and indeed from conversation with Gaelic speakers—it is clear that the developments are widespread. Again the Linguistic Survey will, it is hoped, enable us to plot these developments with much greater accuracy than has been possible in the past. However, it is to be hoped that this promise will not discourage others from research enterprise in this very interesting field. We clearly are in need of studies such as Wigger 1970 on Conamara Irish, not to mention an institution such as the Irish Linguistics Institute to promote relevant study.

Syntax

It is probably the case that syntax is the area of Scottish Gaelic language study that has been most neglected. This is unfortunate because there is no doubt that it is the area that is of most potential interest to general linguists.

Little has been written on the subject. There is some useful material in the early grammars we mentioned above, such as Shaw, Stewart and Calder, and Ó Rahilly 1932 and Fraser 1910, for example, have made interesting comments on specific features. Anderson (1909 and 1910) wrote briefly on the syntax of the 'verbs *to be*' *is* and *tha*. In addition there are brief sections in the dialect monographs we mentioned and there is a lot of material in pedagogic grammars, though it is not very well organised. I wrote an article on the order of elements in clause structure, principally concerned with surface structure relationships (MacAulay 1965), and Ahlqvist 1978 has a great deal of relevant material on the position of adverbials. There is an article on verb complementation (Stenson & Norwood 1975) which contains a fair amount of Scottish Gaelic exemplification (as well as Irish), which is of considerable interest, but suffers somewhat from the writers' lack of a deep knowledge of the language.

There are encouraging signs of an interest in Gaelic by general linguists, and evidence that a fair amount of research is proceeding. These are to be seen in references in work not primarily concerned with Gaelic, such as Comrie 1976 and Anderson 1973. It is most heartening to see this interest, and one hopes that it develops widely. One should, perhaps, add a plea that the examples presented, and especially the implications of the selection of these examples, should be more rigorously checked.

In addition to this, there is interesting work being done which has not yet reached the stage of general publication. Dr David Cram, my colleague in Linguistics in Aberdeen, is engaged in constructing a transformational-generative grammar of Gaelic on 'standard theory' lines; Mr Simpson in Linguistics in Glasgow is looking at some problems in a 'case grammar' of Gaelic; Mr Neil Mitchison is investigating the syntax of the 'verb *to be*' among other things. I, myself, have recently been looking at the syntax of aspectual sentences and the structure of the noun phrase as part of a general syntactic description. In spite of this activity, however, it must be said that in the realm of syntactic investigation Gaelic lags a long way behind other Celtic languages, notably Welsh (cf Jones & Thomas), and Irish, where much interesting work has recently been done (see *Teangeolas*, the publication of the Institiúid Teangeolaíochta, for details).

Vocabulary
The study of meaning in Gaelic is almost entirely confined to

the study of word meaning, and within that field to the making of bilingual dictionaries, though there is a scattering of articles on particular items and some comparative material of interest (cf Ó Rahilly 1932). There are a number of dictionaries available in Gaelic, and many of them are of considerable value. It must be said that they are of more value when one knows the language than when one does not and probably the major criticism one would wish to make of them is that they are grossly short on citation. Dwelly's dictionary (Dwelly 1911) is no doubt the best Gaelic-English one. There is a great lack of any very useful English-Gaelic dictionary, though I am informed that the volume that An Comunn Gaidhealach have had in preparation for many years may soon appear. MacBain 1911 is the only etymological dictionary that can be at all recommended (and there too it helps to know the subject!). Dieckhoff 1932, based on the Gaelic of Glengarry, is the best of the pronouncing dictionaries.

There are supplementary and specialised vocabularies available. Good examples of the former type are Father Allan MacDonald's vocabulary (1958) and the vocabulary in Volume VI of *Carmina Gadelica*. In the latter category we have, for example, Forbes 1905 on the names of animals, birds and fishes, the vocabulary in Derick Thomson's translation of a biology text-book (MacLeoid 1976; cf also Chapter 2) and the lists of technical terms related to office administration and secretarial practice produced in connection with the new Gaelic-based secretarial course established in Lewis Castle College. There are a number of other examples of both kinds, though it must be said that the terminology appropriate for a modern technological society has been very slow in its development in Gaelic and even slower in the standardisation necessary for its firm establishment. Comhairle nan Eilean's bilingual policy (cf Comhairle nan Eilean 1977) will no doubt help to effect this.

As I said at the beginning, one of the two major Gaelic language projects in progress is the dictionary on historical principles being prepared in the Celtic Department of the University of Glasgow. This project is making good progress and will be of tremendous value when it is available, but it is an immense task and will take a long time to complete. Its interim value is already obvious to those of us working in the field of Gaelic studies (see MacDhomhnaill 1977), and we have cause to be grateful to the editor for his unselfish help on numerous occasions.

Comparative
(a) Historical
Non-historical intra-Gaelic comparative work has been looked at when discussing dialect studies. Gaelic dialect studies have mostly been areally based, but intra-language comparison may be based on other dimensions, such as social groups within the population or even age bands (see Mac-Aulay 1978). This will be discussed below in the context of sociolinguistics.

Almost no work has been done overtly on the history of Scottish Gaelic itself. Most of what exists is concerned with the deformation of the classical Scottish Gaelic morphological system (cf Dorian 1973, MacAulay 1978a, Ó Murchú 1975, for exemplification and some comment), though changes in syntax are commented on (MacAulay 1978a) and there are notable changes taking place in the network of relationships between form and function in verb morphology (cf Greene 1973, 129f.).

There is considerable interest at present in the relationship between the earliest forms of Scottish Gaelic and Classical Gaelic. Mr Gillies in the Department of Celtic in Edinburgh and Mr Meek in the Department of Celtic in Glasgow are both working on different aspects of the early sixteenth century *Book of the Dean of Lismore*. Each of them is concerned with establishing texts for this extremely difficult work, and one of the aspects they have to deal with is the extent to which forms are Scottish Gaelic as distinct from Classical Gaelic. Their work promises to be of great interest from the point of view of the history of Gaelic. (See also Thomson 1976.)

Scottish Gaelic has, of course, been compared with the classical language from which in a sense it derives (cf Jackson 1951), though the more one studies Scottish Gaelic the clearer it becomes that some features of it are more archaic than Classical Gaelic norms (at least as known to us now) and must represent a continuity from an earlier date (see Greene 1973). Ó Rahilly 1932 places Gaelic in the context of 'Irish dialects past and present' as does Wagner & Ó Baoill but perhaps the most extensive comparison is that made between Northern Irish and Scottish Gaelic in Ó Baoill 1978.

Our knowledge of the history of Gaelic will be greatly enhanced once the historical dictionary, which we mentioned above, begins to be published.

(*b*) *Contact with other languages*

In its history in Scotland, Gaelic has been in contact with other languages—as a look at the distribution of Gaelic- and other-language-based place-names in Scotland, for instance, makes clear to us (and cf Murison 1974; Mackinnon 1974; Campbell 1950). These languages have left their imprint on Gaelic, though it must once again be admitted that our knowledge of even such comparatively retrievable kinds of information as the percentages of exotic items in Gaelic vocabulary is sadly imprecise.

Gaelic contains many words of Latin origin. Most of these are early borrowings which Gaelic has in common with Irish and the majority have (or had) to do with religious domains. For instance, one hundred and thirteen words cited as Latin borrowings in *Cormac's Glossary* (late ninth century) are extant still in my dialect, and these represent only a small proportion of the items of Latin origin.

There are a fair number of general words from Norse, as one would expect, but according to Oftedal 1962b there are surprisingly few core vocabulary words, most items belonging to special terminologies such as those of ships and seafaring. There is no organised list of Norse borrowings in Gaelic such as Bugge 1912 (but see Henderson 1910, chapter V).

Gaelic borrowings from its Pictish and Cumbric neighbours in Scotland are few, as far as one can see. The same, certainly nowadays, and in substantial numbers back to the seventeenth century, cannot be said of borrowings from English. Again, however there is little published data (but see Watson 1927, Oftedal 1962b). The evidence is plain to see in both the written and spoken word. The state of Gaelic-English bilingualism is now such that words are normally borrowed by Gaelic speakers without any attempt being made to adjust their sounds or their forms to the appropriate Gaelic system. Indeed obvious borrowings which in the past have been given a Gaelic form now have their original English form reinstated in many cases (see MacAulay 1978).

Borrowings are fairly easy to identify but there are other influences arising from contact which are much more controversial. For example the syntax of aspectually marked sentences in Gaelic and Welsh (cf Awbery 1976) are very similar and it is tempting to suppose that the similarity has to do with the influence of Brittonic on Gaelic, but such a contention is almost impossible to prove. Similarities, especially in the sound system, have been noticed between Gaelic and Norse (Borgstrøm 1974; Oftedal 1962b) and these have been discussed in terms of sub-stratum and typology (Marstrander 1932; Oftedal 1968; Wagner 1964). Similarities between Gaelic and English syntax have been noted also (MacAulay 1978; Wagner 1959), but a great deal more research would be required before one could make final judgments on this. What has recently become clear, expecially with the development of studies in linguistic typology, is that scholars are more cautious in their assignment of linguistic influences—and this is, without doubt, the sensible line to take.

Social Dimensions
There has recently been considerable interest in this field. The social dimensions of language are many and probably most of the work done in this area by Dr K M MacKinnon, for example, would be best classified as the sociology of language. He has looked at the history of Gaelic in Scotland (MacKinnon 1974), at the way in which it correlates with education and other social processes (MacKinnon 1977) and at how it operates institutionally in Scotland (MacKinnon, K M 1971). The work of such as Campbell 1950, MacLeod 1963 and most of the contents of MacThómais 1976, and of many others dealing with the same field in a less academic fashion, could be classified in the same terms.

More concerned with actual language forms and functions are MacAulay 1978 and MacLeod 1976. MacAulay Forthcoming b deals with problems such as diglossia, domain usage, code-switching and in general aspects of register range and choice. This is a field which seems at present to be capturing the interest of a fair number of scholars. Dorian Forthcoming deals with the problems of language loyalty and language status in different groups in Mull (cf ILAR 1975).

The most extensive and the most convincing psycholinguistic study relating to Gaelic is Dr F MacLeod's investigation into bilingualism (MacLeod 1969). Earlier studies such as Smith 1948 and Vernon 1965 had dealt with the problems of intelligence testing and the correlation of ability and achievement in the cultural complex of the Western Isles, on a smaller scale. Now that a bilingual policy in education is established in that area, one looks forward to the development of investigations geared with a new linguistic relevance to determining the nature of local educational needs.

Pedagogic Language Materials

With the increased interest in the learning of Gaelic at different age levels and in different institutional situations in recent years, there has been an increasing demand for language learning materials. And indeed in some areas, notably materials for young children, for use in school, and elementary material for beginners, these have been forthcoming.

Children's material has been produced for both learners and native speakers (formerly the latter often remained illiterate in their own language, of course; see Inverness Report 1955; Inverness Scheme 1964) and there is no doubt that this material is a great improvement on what had previously been available. The same is true of the new learners' material being produced. There is also, now, more variety available. MacKinnon, R 1971 is a self-instructional course; Ferguson n.d. and MacDhomhnaill, I A 1976 are both supported by useful oral/aural materials. There is no doubt that the latter is the most sophisticated material publicly available at the present time for Gaelic learning purposes, and that the author's long experience in this field of endeavour has stood him in good stead (see, for example, MacDonald 1968).

As well as these published materials, one knows of several additional efforts by individuals and groups of teachers that are already or will soon be at the publication stage. These derive from the school situation, from evening class work and from the universities, where all the Departments of Celtic now run their own learners' classes and produce their own additional support material.

Generally, there is more activity in this field and probably more direction than there has ever been (both in Gaelic and non-Gaelic areas). There is a great deal however to be done. One can see perhaps three major shortcomings in the material available. Looked at from a professional point of view, courses tend not to be sufficiently directed to a defined population, and this in the future will have to be rectified. In the second place there is a great dearth of second and third stage advanced material; and in the third place there is a lack of a good grammar reference source. This last deficiency has been helped a bit by Blacklaw 1978, but only at the early stages and to a limited degree. It is also clear that supportive and coordinative administrative structures are urgently needed.

This paper has come back on several occasions to the comment that much requires to be done in the field of Gaelic language studies, and that too little is being done. In spite of the evidence for considerable interest and activity in many areas of the subject at present, it seems to me that anyone looking at the situation dispassionately would find that conclusion unavoidable. It would be appropriate then to conclude with some brief remarks on what would seem to be crucial conditions for advance in the areas which we have discussed.

Nothing has been said here of the place of Gaelic in the media, in the education or administrative systems, in the church, or in less formal institutions, as this is dealt with elsewhere. However, the status of Gaelic in these institutions is a crucial factor, and we need to have a definition of it and a clear idea of what we require it to be. There are, then, basic studies to be done on these topics.

There are, for example, important demographic facts in the situation. The Census of 1971 as compared with that of 1961 (see Census 1966; Census 1975) shows interesting developments in the distribution of Gaelic speakers in Scotland: an increase of around 8 000 speakers instead of the expected decrease, this increase being outwith the traditional Gaelic areas. This distributional shift needs to be investigated in detail and its implications considered for the future place of Gaelic in Scotland. (The same might be said of the reactions of the Registrar General's office, which canvassed the suggestion that Gaelic statistical questions might in future be drastically reduced!) For example, Gaelic media provision on a network and community basis are subjects for urgent study. Blanket percentage figures are irrelevant to actual needs.

In education, administrative structures are badly needed to support the new developments at school level. There is no curriculum committee on Gaelic, for example, and this means that the sort of central guidance and often the financial backing available to other subjects at this level are lacking, with the result that activities are unco-ordinated and badly funded.

At University level developments in the subject have not been supported by administrative structures or funding either. They have been made possible by teachers increasing their commitment to face-to-face teaching, often to a level which is quite unacceptable if they are to promote, administer and actually do the research that, as I've pointed out, needs to be done. There are too few people doing too many things, and the universities in Scotland (and the Colleges of Education also) ought to recognise their responsibilities in this sphere a good deal more readily than they have done in the past.

Finally, there is an urgent need for a Gaelic Language Institute, on the lines of the Irish Linguistic Institute in Dublin, for example, to promote and coordinate language-based work in Gaelic of all kinds. The success of the Irish set-up shows the contribution that such an institution can make, with official backing and fairly modest funding, to the organisation and rationalisation of this area of related studies. We should direct our best endeavours to establish its equivalent in Scotland.

Bibliography to Chapter 7

Ahlqvist, A 1978. On preposed adverbials *Scottish Gaelic Studies [SGS]* 13, 66–80.
Anderson, A O 1909. The syntax of copula *is* in modern Scottish Gaelic *Zeitschrift für Celtische Philologie [ZCP]* 7, 439–449.
Anderson, A O 1910. The syntax of the substantive verb *tha* in modern Scottish Gaelic *ZCP* 8, 236–241.
Anderson, J 1973. *An Essay Concerning Aspect.* The Hague: Mouton.
Awbery, G M 1976. *The Syntax of Welsh.* Cambridge University Press.
Blacklaw, B 1978. *Bun-chùrsa Gaidhlig.* Roinn nan Cànan Ceilteach, Oilthigh Ghlaschu.
Bonaparte, Prince L-L 1882. Initial mutations in the living Celtic, Basque, Sardinian and Italian dialects *Transactions of the Philological Society* 1882-4, 155–202.
Borgstrøm, C Hj 1937. The dialect of Barra in the Outer Hebrides *Norsk Tidsskrift for Sprogvidenskap [NTS]* 7, 71–224.
Borgstrøm, C Hj 1940. *The Dialects of the Outer Hebrides. NTS* Supplement Bind 1. Oslo.
Borgstrøm, C Hj 1941. *The Dialects of Skye and Ross-shire. NTS* Supplement Bind 2. Oslo.
Borgstrøm, C Hj 1974. On the influence of Norse on Scottish Gaelic *Lochlann* 6, 91–103.
Bugge, A 1912. Norse loan words in Irish. In O S Bergin & C

Marstrander (eds) *Miscellany presented to Kuno Meyer*, 291–306. Halle: Niemeyer.

Calder, G 1923. *A Gaelic Grammar.* Glasgow: MacLaren.

Campbell, J L 1948. Scottish Gaelic in Canada *An Gaidheal* 43.

Campbell, J L 1950. *Gaelic in Scottish Education and Life.* Edinburgh: W A & K Johnston.

Carmina Gadelica 1971. *Carmina Gadelica by Alexander Carmichael*, vol VI (ed A Matheson). Edinburgh: Scottish Academic Press.

Carmody, F J 1945. The interrogative system in modern Scottish Gaelic *University of California Publications in Linguistics* 1, 6, 215–226.

Census 1966. *Census of Scotland 1961* vol VII. Edinburgh: HMSO.

Census 1975. *Census of Scotland 1971: Gaelic Report.* Edinburgh: HMSO.

Comhairle nan Eilean 1977. *The Bilingual Policy: a Consultative Document.* Stornoway: Council Offices.

Comrie, B 1976. *Aspect: an Introduction to the Study of Verbal Aspect and Related Problems.* Cambridge University Press.

Cram, D 1975. Grammatical and phonological conditioning of initial mutations in Scottish Gaelic *Leuvense Bijdagen* 64, 363–375.

Dieckhoff, H C 1932. *Pronouncing Dictionary of Scottish Gaelic based on the Dialect of the Glengarry District.* Edinburgh.

Dorian, N 1973. Grammatical change in a dying dialect. *Language* 49, 413–438.

Dorian, N 1976. Gender in a terminal Gaelic dialect *SGS* 12, 279–282.

Dorian, N 1978. *East Sutherland Gaelic: The Dialect of Brora, Golspie, and Embo Fishing Communities.* Dublin: Institute for Advanced Studies.

Dorian, N Forthcoming. The valuation of Gaelic by different mother-tongue groups resident in the Highlands (to appear in *SGS* 13, 2).

Dwelly, E 1911. *The Illustrated Gaelic Dictionary* Herne Bay.

Ellis, J O 1965. The grammatical status of initial mutation *Lochlann* 3, 315–330.

Ferguson, C (n.d.) *Sàth: A Gaelic Teaching Course.* Glasgow: Caledonian Music Co.

Forbes, A R 1905. *Gaelic Names of Beasts, Birds, Fishes etc.* Edinburgh.

Fraser, J 1910. The relative clause in Scottish Gaelic *Celtic Review* 6, 356 f.

Fraser, J 1923. Grammatical notes on Scottish Gaelic, I and II *Revue Celtique* 40, 137–142; 41, 189–195.

Greene, D 1973. Synthetic and analytic: a reconsideration *Ériu* 24, 121–133.

Gunn, A 1889. The dialect of the Reay Country *Transactions of the Gaelic Society of Inverness [TGSI]* 15 (1888–1889), 35f.

134 *Languages of Scotland*

Hamp, E P 1951. Morphophonemes of the Keltic mutations *Language* **27**, 230–247.

Henderson, G 1910. *The Norse Influence on Celtic Scotland* Glasgow: Maclehose.

Holmer, N M 1938. Studies in Argyllshire Gaelic. *Skrifta utgivna av K. humanistica Vetenskap Samfundet i Uppsala* **31** (1938–9).

Holmer, N M 1957. *The Gaelic of Arran*. Dublin: Institute for Advanced Studies.

Holmer, N M 1962. *The Gaelic of Kintyre*. Dublin: Institute for Advanced Studies.

ILAR 1975. *Report of the Committee on Irish Language Attitudes Research*. Baile Atha Cliath.

Inverness Report 1955. *Report on Teaching of Gaelic*. Inverness-shire Education Committee.

Inverness Scheme 1964. *Scheme of Instruction in Gaelic*. Inverness County Council Education Dept.

Jackson, K H 1951. *Common Gaelic: The Evolution of the Goedelic Languages*. London: Rhŷs Memorial Lecture.

Jackson, K H 1967. Palatalization of Labials in the Gaelic Languages. In W Meid (ed) *Beiträge zur Indogermanistik und Keltologie*, 179–192.

Jones, M & Thomas, A R 1978. *The Welsh Language: Studies in its Syntax and Semantics*. Cardiff: University of Wales Press.

MacAulay, D 1962. Notes on some noun-initial mutations in a dialect of Scottish Gaelic *SGS* **9**, 2, 146–178.

MacAulay, D 1965. A grammatical approach to *is* and related problems *SGS* **10**, 216–234.

MacAulay, D 1966. Palatalisation of labials in Scottish Gaelic and some related problems in phonology *SGS* **11**, 72–84.

MacAulay, D 1978. Intra-dialectal variation as an aspect of Gaelic linguistic research *SGS* **13**, 81–97.

MacAulay, D 1979. Some functional and distributional aspects of intonation in Scottish Gaelic: a preliminary study of tones. [Plenary paper given at Congress on Celtic Phonology, Coleraine, June 1977; to be published in Proceedings of Congress; in press.]

MacAulay, D Forthcoming a. The placement of nuclear tone in Gaelic response sentences. [Paper given to Aberdeen Linguistics Seminar, March 1978; to be published in *SGS* **13**, 2.]

MacAulay, D Forthcoming b. Some aspects of register range and choice in Scottish Gaelic. In J Ellis and J N Ure (eds) *International Journal of the Sociology of Language: Register Range and Change Issue*. [In press.]

MacBain, A 1892. The dialect of Badenoch *TGSI* **18**, 79–96.

MacBain, A 1911. *An Etymological Dictionary of the Gaelic Language*. Stirling: Eneas Mackay.

MacDhomhnaill, C D 1977. A' Trusadh dhan an Fhaclair *Gairm* **97**, 74–77.

MacDhomhnaill, I A 1976. *Gàidhlig Bheò* vols 1–4. Cambridge: National Extension College.

MacDonald, Fr A 1958. *Gaelic Words & Expressions from South Uist and Eriskay* (ed J L Campbell). Dublin: Institute for Advanced Studies.

MacDonald, J A 1968. *Ceum air Cheum: a New Approach to Gaelic.* Glasgow.

MacGill-Fhinnein, G 1966. *Gàidhlig Uidhist a Deas.* Institiúid Árd-Leínn Bhaile Atha Cliath.

MacInnes, J 1973. Some Gaelic words and usages *TGSI* **49**, 428–455.

MacKinnon, K M 1971. *A Sociological Study of Scottish Gaelic as an Institution in Scottish Life and Education* Unpublished M A dissertation, London University Institute of Education.

MacKinnon, K M 1972. Education and social control: the case of Gaelic Scotland. In *Scottish Education Studies* **4**, no 2.

MacKinnon, K M 1974. *The Lion's Tongue.* Inverness: Club Leabhar.

MacKinnon, K M 1977. *Language, Education and Social Process in a Gaelic Community.* London: Routledge & Kegan Paul.

MacKinnon, R 1971. *Gaelic: Teach Yourself Books.* London: English Universities Press.

MacLeod, D J 1976. A' Ghàidlig am Beatha fhollaiseach an t-Sluaigh. In MacThómais, R (Deas) *Gàidhlig ann an Albainn,* 12–27.

MacLeod, F 1969. *Experimental Investigations into Some Problems of Bilingualism.* Unpublished Ph D thesis, University of Aberdeen.

MacLeod, M 1963. Gaelic in Highland Education *TGSI* **43**, 305–334.

MacLeòid, R 1976. *Bith-eòlas: A' Chealla, Ginntinneachd is Meanfhas.* (Eader R MacThómais). Glaschu: Gairm Publications.

MacThómais, R (Deas) 1976. *Gáidhlig ann an Albainn.* Glaschu: Gairm Publications.

Marstrander, C 1932. Okklusiver og substrater *NTS* **5**, 258–314.

Murison, D 1974. Linguistic relationships in mediaeval Scotland. In G W S Barrow (ed) *The Scottish Tradition: Essays in Honour of R G Cant.* Edinburgh: Scottish Academic Press.

Ó Baoill, C 1978. *Contributions to a Comparative Study of Ulster Irish and Scottish Gaelic.* Belfast: Institute of Irish Studies, Queen's University.

Ó Dochartaigh, C Forthcoming. Phonology of the Gaelic Liquids. [Paper given to Aberdeen Linguistics Seminar April 1978; to appear in *SGS* **13**, 2.]

Oftedal, M 1956. *The Gaelic of Leurbost NTS* Supplement Bind IV. Oslo.

Oftedal, M 1962a. A morphemic evaluation of the Celtic initial mutations *Lochlann* **2**, 93–102.

Oftedal, M 1962b. On the frequency of Norse loanwords in Scottish Gaelic *SGS* **9**, 116–127.

Oftedal, M 1963. On 'palatalised' labials in Scottish Gaelic *SGS* 10, 71–81.

Oftedal, M 1968. North European geography of sounds *SGS* 11, 248–258.

Ó Murchú, M 1970. *Urlabhra agus Pobal* Paípéar Ocáidiúil 1, Comhairle na Gaeilge.

Ó Murchú, M 1976. The article in a variety of Perthshire Gaelic *Celtica* 11, 187–193.

Ó Rahilly, T F 1932. *Irish Dialects Past and Present.* Dublin: Browne & Nolan.

Robertson, C M 1906–1909. Scottish Gaelic dialects *Celtic Review* 3, 97f; 4, 69f; 5, 79f.

Rogers, H 1972. The initial mutations in Modern Scottish Gaelic *Celtica* 7, 63–85.

SCRE 1961. Scottish Council for Research in Education, *Gaelic-speaking Children in Highland Schools.* University of London Press.

Shaw, W 1778. *An Analysis of the Gaelic Language.* London. Reprinted by the Scolar Press, Menston, 1972.

Shuken, C 1977. *Aspiration in Scottish Gaelic Stop Consonants* [Paper read at IPS 77: an International Phonetics Sciences Congress, Miami Beach.]

Smith, C A 1948. *Mental Testing of Hebridean Children.* SCRE Publication No XLVII. Edinburgh.

Stenson, S & Norwood, S 1975. Aspect and complementation in q-Celtic. In *Papers from the 11th Regional Meeting of the Chicago Linguistic Society.* University of Chicago Department of Linguistics.

Stewart, A 1801. *Elements of Gaelic Grammar.* Edinburgh.

Ternes, E 1973. *The Phonemic Analysis of Scottish Gaelic.* Forum Phoneticum 1. Hamburg: Helmut Buske Verlag.

Thomson, R L 1976. The language of the Caogad. *SGS* 12, 143–182.

Vernon, P E 1965. Abilities and attainments in the Western Isles *Scottish Educational Journal,* 8 October 1965.

Wagner, H 1959. *Das Verbum in den Sprachen der Britischen Inseln: ein Beitrag zur geographischen Typologie des Verbums.* Tübingen: Niemayer.

Wagner, H 1964. Nordeuropäische Lautgeographie *ZCP* 29, 225–298.

Wagner, H & Ó Baoill, C 1969. *Linguistic Atlas and Survey of Irish Dialects,* vol IV. Dublin: Institute for Advanced Studies.

Watson, J 1974. A Gaelic dialect of N E Ross-shire *Lochlann* 6, 9f.

Watson, W J 1927. Some interactions between Gaelic and English *TGSI* 33, 310–326.

Wigger, A 1970. *Nominalformen in Conamara-Irischen.* Hamburg: Lüdke.

Wigger, A & Ó Siadhail, M 1975. *Córas Fuaimeanna na Gaeilge.* Institiúid Ard-Léinn Bhaile Atha Cliath.

8
Studies on Scots and Scottish Standard English today

A J Aitken

On 20 November 1971, I was, with David Murison and Hans Speitel, one of those who addressed the second one-day conference of the then infant Association for Scottish Literary Studies (ASLS)[1]. That conference, attended by about one hundred and twenty people, was the first ever to be held on the subject of 'The Scottish Language'. By this its organisers meant only one of the three considered in this book—Scots. The general tenor of my state-of-play report (Aitken 1972a) on recent work on Scots was that there was little enough to report on, barring the large dictionaries and the Linguistic Survey; that nearly all of what there was took place in Edinburgh; and that university and other teaching of Scots was far from copious.

I can now report quite a striking expansion in informed interest in, and research on, Scots, even though the increase in the number of university teaching posts I had hoped for has not materialised.

Some of this expansion was a direct outcome of the 1971 conference itself. In its final session the conference elected a committee to continue fostering interest in Scots language as a subject of study, and this committee became what is now the Language Committee of the ASLS. One useful achievement of this Committee has been to run a series of conferences and also to help to instigate and to take part in two in-service College of Education courses on Scots language, up and down the country, from Berwick to Thurso. These, and other, conferences and courses, and publications resulting from them, are listed on pp 158–160 below.

The ASLS is of course not the only voluntary body which is active in fostering interest in Scots. Some, including the Saltire Society and the Federation of Burns Clubs, have been doing so for many years. A comparative newcomer which, like the ASLS, has Scots language as a central concern, is the Lallans Society, subsequently re-named the Scots Language Society. This society furthers one of its principal aims—that of 'promoting Scots as a language'—by the publication of a twice-yearly magazine *Lallans* (1973–), largely written in traditional or literary Scots, what William Grant and James Main Dixon in their *Manual of Modern Scots* (Cambridge University Press, 1921) xxi–xxii, called Standard Scots. Beginning with *Lallans* 3, (Mairtinmas 1974), William Graham has contributed a series of 'Lessons', first in English entitled 'Teach yourself Lallans', subsequently (from number 7, Mairtinmas 1976) in Lallans, entitled 'Teach yourself Scots'. Mr Graham has now produced a book to this end (Graham 1977).

Numerous occasional pieces on aspects of Scots appear from time to time in Scottish (and occasionally English) newspapers and magazines, including specialist literary magazines such as *Scotia Review* and *Akros*. The latter's Scots Language Issue, April 1977, included an interesting paper by Lorna Borrowman on 'The Scots tongue in education' (Borrowman 1977), originally delivered on 5 June 1976 to the Scots Language Society's fifth Annual Conference. Miss Borrowman investigated by questionnaire the teaching of Scots language and literature in twelve schools, including some from both urban and rural areas. The extent to which teaching of Scots was carried out varied widely but in none of the schools investigated was no Scots literature read. Her paper does not make it clear whether all schools did this in every class from S1 to S6, but at least one, Garnock Academy in Ayrshire, evidently did, the Fifth and Sixth Year classes there taking in recent drama such as *Willie Rough* and *The Sash*. Two schools said they linked the study of Scots poetry with a course in the development of the Lowland Scots language, and two studied dialect variation. Two schools stated that they did not discourage pupils from speaking dialect in class, though none admitted to encouraging this. Garnock Academy's English Department does indeed run a sustained course over six years in Scots Literature and Language. And Scottish Language is one of the five-week options in Edinburgh Royal High School's courses in Scottish Studies given to its Third, Fourth and Fifth Forms.

Miss Borrowman's findings complement those of John Low. Dr Low's investigations were carried out through visits to schools and conversations with many teachers in the Lothian area in 1974. Dr Low reported that though many Scots—teachers and others—regarded Scots speech, especially urban working-class speech, as hardly respectable, either for communication or as a topic of study, a modicum of Scots literature was being taught in many schools, 'with little official encouragement, but often with the active encouragement of head teachers' (Low 1974, 19).

It is not my own impression that there is in Scottish schools today much classroom discussion of the history of the language, or its present situation, or why certain usages are stigmatised and others not, and the other problems in this area which I suggested as topics in my essay on Scots Language in the report *Scottish Literature in the Secondary School* (Aitken 1976, 52–55). And many teachers apparently still believe, despite the arguments of the sociolinguists, that to permit Scots speech in class will inhibit the successful learning of English. All the same, both Miss Borrowman and Dr Low reveal a lot of interest in and *some* teaching of Scots language today in schools and at least one training college, and that is much more than was the case not too long ago. Also, I was a little surprised and naturally pleased that the ideas in my own essay that I have just mentioned seemed to meet such enthusiastic approbation as they did from several writers in the Scottish educational press. I advocated tolerance of all varieties of Scots speech, including the generally stigmatised varieties, and urged the importance of its study as a concern of Scots pupils.

These views are very different from the opinions on Scots speech and how to treat it presented in the Scottish Education Department reports on *Primary Education in Scotland* 1946 and on *English in Secondary Schools* 1952; in these, 'genuine dialect' which, however, 'could not be described as a suitable medium of education and culture', is held to exist only in rural areas, but elsewhere, it is said, this has 'sadly degenerated, and become a worthless jumble of slipshod, ungrammatical and vulgar forms'. Attitudes like this do seem to be giving way to what I should regard as more liberal and enlightened ones among Scottish educationalists, including educational administrators, educational journalists and teachers in all tiers of the system.

As Dr Low and Miss Borrowman pointed out, Scottish teachers often complain of the dearth of moderately priced and available published literature of all genres in Scots, suitable for classroom use. To help remedy this, the Scottish Materials in Schools Committee, based on the English

Departments of Hamilton and Craigie Colleges of Education, is at work on the production of a kit for primary school use, in association with the Centre of Information for the Teaching of English. An anthology of Scottish primary schoolchildren's rhymes, songs, lore and writing has been assembled by Mr Graham Stephen and was recently published by Oliver and Boyd.[2] Two anthologies of Scottish writing directed to primary schools are expected to appear in 1979, published by Collins. An extensive list of books, films and recordings in Scots, suitable for school use, forms part of the report *Scottish Literature in the Secondary School* referred to above.[3]

We are today far better provided with specimens of fictitious but plausibly realistic Scots dialogue in a range of varieties than we have been up to about the beginning of the present decade—in poetry especially by poets of the Glasgow 'Toonheid vernacular' (or Glasgow Demotic) school[4], by authors of novels, short stories, monologues[5], sociological reports[6], and drama[7], and numerous books of reminiscence from various airts, such as those of Cliff Hanley and Molly Weir on Glasgow.

Publicly available recordings of unscripted speech in the Scots vernacular remain almost non-existent (there is a little in *English with a Dialect*, BBC Records, REC 173), though of course there are large collections in the archives of the Linguistic Survey of Scotland (Scots Section), the Department of Linguistics and the School of Scottish Studies, all of Edinburgh University; and specimens can also now be collected readily from broadcast phone-in programmes especially of Radio Forth and Radio Clyde. Once the School of Scottish Studies publishes its promised record of specimens of Scottish folk-tales, no doubt this will also illustrate some Scots dialects and accents. For vocal recordings of specimens of Scots literature of every date, see first *Scottish Literature in the Secondary School* pp 105–111, and also the cassette recordings published by Scotsoun[8] and Scotsway[9], and Adam McNaughtan's record of his own and traditional songs.[10] For no doubt somewhat stereotyped material in rural varieties, records and/or cassettes by Rhoda Butler (from Shetland) and Flora Garry (from Aberdeenshire) are now available. Glasgow speech, more or less heavily stereotyped, is imitated or reproduced in records by well-known Scots comics such as Stanley Baxter and Billy Connolly.

All that I have so far written appears to manifest an interest in the Lowland Scots language which has very recently strikingly increased. This enhancement of interest stands in a chicken-and-egg relationship to the work of bodies like the ASLS and the Scots Language Society. So far, this increased interest has not spilled over to any great extent into broadcasting exposure, where vernacular speech is heard little more often than it ever was, and only as a couthy, folksy, *genre* interlude within the more serious and normal material in Standard English. As yet this barrier to a re-Scotticisation of Lowland speech has remained firmly up. Yet press correspondence on matters to do with vernacular speech does seem more often well-informed and liberal than it was twenty years or so ago, and it is perhaps another sign of the times that the broadcasting media appear to grant rather greater tolerance to non-RP accents than was once the case, albeit in this they are perhaps following a current social trend rather than leading it.

None of the work mentioned above which has helped to foster interest in the Scots tongue has been at any cost to the public purse. What of the publicly maintained institutions of learning themselves? A little has already been said of what appears to be the trend in schools—still a matter of private enthusiasm by individual school heads and teachers with little official encouragement (such as might be given by more overt inclusion of Scottish language topics in the examination syllabuses). The members of English staffs in the Colleges of Education whom I myself know are extremely well-informed on and well-disposed to the kind of approach to Scots as a speech and as a subject which I believe in myself. But given the limited hours of student contact they have, the amount of actual teaching time they can give to the subject can not be expected to be large. I do not doubt however that more liberal attitudes to all varieties of Scottish speech are now being fostered in College of Education English Departments.

In the universities, there is as yet only one full-time teaching post specifically assigned to Lowland Scots language in the world, the Lectureship in Scots Language held in the University of Glasgow by Janet Templeton till her untimely death three years ago and since occupied by David Murison. The latter's work includes a course on the history of Scots of two periods per week over three years to honours students of Scottish Literature; he also gives a short course on the same topic of one period weekly over one term within the English Language Department.

In the University of Edinburgh there are courses in Scottish Literature and in Oral Tradition whose students make some acquaintance with vernacular Scots. First-year students of English Language learn something of the phonetics of Scottish Standard English, of Scots (and English) regional dialects, and are given a brief overview of the sociolinguistic situation in Scotland; second-year students study Older Scots linguistically and stylistically; and each year a few students—classes of about eight are normal—take a third and fourth year specialist course leading to a Final Honours paper on the History of Lowland Scots. The third year part of this course is on the secondary literature and resources, the history, the history of sounds and on Older Scots texts. The fourth year has optional sections, including pre-literary Scots, the language of Older Scots poetry, modern Scots in literature, regional and social variation in modern Scots, and, since 1976/77, the place-names of Scotland. Except in Glasgow, most of these topics have never before been taught anywhere to anything like the same intensiveness; and the place-names option is a world first. Scots data also figures prominently in some of the courses taught in Edinburgh's Department of Linguistics.

Except in Glasgow and Edinburgh, the study of Scots and Scottish Standard English figures much less prominently or not at all in English courses. Only in Aberdeen is some time specifically committed to this, taught at present by J Derrick McClure, but less than in the south. A reading of the Calendars of Queen's University, Belfast, or of the New University of Ulster, does not indicate that much time, if any, is given in undergraduate courses to the Scots language from which the local speech there partly descends, though members of these universities and others in Ulster are currently very active in research on the regional and social dialectologies of Ulster speech. There are also a few other universities widely dispersed round the world where expatriate Scots or native Scotophiles improve the local English or Linguistics curricula with a few classes devoted to Older Scots or the modern Scots dialects.

All this may sound disappointing, especially after what I was able to say about what seems to be a new extra-mural enthusiasm for the study of Scots, but we should remember that even so the situation is far better than it was only a few years ago. For example, Glasgow's Honours Scots Literature course is only six or seven years old, and Edinburgh's Honours Lowland Scots course dates only from 1969.

In new research there is much more happening and a more promising outlook than there was in 1971. It is however still fair comment, as it was in 1971, that most of it, one way or another, has an Edinburgh University address, though it should also be remembered that two of the major enterprises—the large dictionaries—were and, in the case of the *Dictionary of the Older Scottish Tongue*, still are managed and supported by not one but seven or, since 1977, six of the Scottish Universities jointly.[11]

The great historical event of recent years has of course been the completion in 1976 of *The Scottish National Dictionary*, thanks most of all to the heroic scholarship of David Murison.

It is right for David Murison and for all his colleagues and for the individuals and institutions who supported his work to feel a sense of great achievement to have the dictionary completed. But it is also an error to think that with the completion of the *SND* the lexicography of modern Scots is finally accomplished. Because the dictionary is finished, that does not mean that the language remains fixed and unchanging. New words and new meanings of words continue to arise in Scotland just as they do in other parts of the English-speaking world like Australia and South Africa, where, incidentally, national dictionaries are also being prepared for. Already some of these new items have come too late for the *SND*—for instance, *to be up to high doh about something*, or *to stay in a scheme* or *in a multy*. And the seventies have produced a flourishing new literature of intentionally realistic colloquial Scots, also too late for the *SND*. Before long we will have to think of a new Supplement to the *SND* on the lines of Robert Burchfield's *Supplement to the Oxford English Dictionary*. Anyone who is inspired to collect word-of-mouth or literary examples for this Supplement and wants a clearing house for the collections should send them to the Scottish National Dictionary Association, 27 George Square, Edinburgh EH8, to be housed along with the materials of the new *Concise Scots Dictionary* (*CSD*), on which the Association is now engaged.

This new venture, *CSD*, is to be a one-volume historical

dictionary digested out of the large dictionaries, *SND* and the *Dictionary of the Older Scottish Tongue*. The editing of this has now (1978) been under way for three years and about thirty-seven per cent of the alphabet is done.

At the time of revision of this paper (1978), the *DOST* had published to Pa, and its present staff of one full-time and two part-time editors and one clerical assistant are working steadily on P, R and S (with P and Q nearly completed). But unless the staff can be expanded, completion of this work, based on 1 500 000 citations, of which 450 000 remain to be edited, cannot be hoped for before the 1990s.

Three years ago the Linguistic Survey of Scotland (Scots Section) began harvesting the results of its twenty-five years of collection with the publication of Volume 1 of the *Linguistic Atlas of Scotland* (Mather & Speitel 1975). This volume and Volume 2 (published in 1977) are both concerned with the regional distributions of words. The results of the phonological survey, which will be Volume 3, may be expected notably to reshape theories and revise preconceptions on the phonological history of Scots, and also to have illuminations to offer for the theorists of the initiation and diffusion of sound change.

In my 1971 talk I suggested that the study of Scots was something of a backwater to the main stream of the linguistics of English, except only in the traditional Scottish strongholds of lexicography and dialectology. Today it is becoming prominent in other ways as well. Hitherto Scots phenomena have been virtually totally ignored by historians of, and commentators on, the *English* language. Now that Roger Lass has made the point that the old British dialects are likely to be at least as informative on the historical phonology of English as the new American ones and has begun citing Scots data fairly copiously, for example in his recent book on English historical phonology (Lass 1976), and Michael Samuels to some extent also (Samuels 1972, e.g. 99; 104–106), Scots may become less of a backwater in this respect. It is to be hoped that the *Linguistic Atlas*'s potential contribution to this will not go unnoticed either.

Then, whereas the University of Leeds's Survey of English Dialects, carried out between 1948 and 1961, stopped short precisely at the Border, the University of Sheffield's new British Urban Linguistic Survey has Scotland as well as England and Ireland on its map.[12]

This brings me to another field in which Scots has recently and suddenly become noticeable—namely, in sociolinguistics or, more precisely, social dialectology, the study of linguistic variation in the social and social-stylistic dimension. In its modern form this branch of linguistics only got going in the early 1960s in the USA, but it is now an important specialism for many linguists all over the world, and of course for some educationalists as well. Though Peter Trudgill's sociolinguistic study of Norwich was actually an Edinburgh Ph D of 1971,[13] the first sociolinguistic investigation of a Scottish situation was Ronald Macaulay's and Gavin Trevelyan's investigation of *Language, Education and Employment in Glasgow* carried out in the first half of 1973 (Macaulay & Trevelyan 1973). Since then two other investigations into sociolinguistic aspects of the speech of Edinburgh schoolchildren have been completed (Romaine 1975a, Reid 1976a), both from Edinburgh's Linguistics Department, and several others are under way or projected, from the Departments of Linguistics or English Language of Edinburgh University and elsewhere.[14] Three of the essays in Trudgill 1978 are on Scottish topics (Macaulay 1978, Reid 1978 and Romaine 1978). The only surprising thing about all this is that it has not happened before, for the linguistic situation in Lowland Scotland offers a remarkably wide and varied range of social dialect phenomena, and a splendid collection of entrenched stereotypes and strongly held traditional attitudes, and the historical background to all of this is unusually well documented here.[15]

Of recent writings on other aspects of Lowland Scots studies the most fundamentally important, in the sense that it is partly a large collection of original data, is Beat Glauser's book on the Scots-English Linguistic Border (Glauser 1974), which helps a great deal to make good the Survey of English Dialect's failure to peek over the frontier. Among much else, Glauser helps to substantiate that the political Border *is* also a very important linguistic border as well, something that we had previously known only intuitively, if at all, though of course Hans Speitel's 1969 article pointed in the same direction (Speitel 1969b).

Apart from all this and apart from what is in *Lowland Scots* (Aitken 1973a) and *The Scots Language in Education* (McClure 1974a) and the other writings already mentioned, the last few years have also seen a number of worthwhile essay-articles and one Ph D thesis on aspects of the past history and present state of Scots. Topics range from pre-fifteenth-century Scots through Older Scots to modern Scots English and Scots dialect theory and George Douglas Brown's use of dialect (for details see the Bibliography under e.g. Aitken, McClure, Mackay, Murison, Speitel). No doubt this kind of thing will continue.[16] Also, two of the desiderata people have long been asking for—a book-length history of Scots and a linguistic reader or series of readers—are now at least contemplated or have an author (David Murison in the case of the first of these, J Derrick McClure for the second) committed to doing them.

On Scottish place-names, we now have W F H Nicolaisen's gathering up of his researches of some seventeen years in his *Scottish Place-Names* (Nicolaisen 1976). These however represent the fruits of earlier rather than current research. The only on-going research into Scottish place-names that I am aware of is Ian Fraser of the Scottish Place-Name Archive's work on the collection of minor names from local oral tradition. In this he has successfully enlisted the very active help of forty branches of the SWRI from all over Scotland and of five local history societies. These will obviously make important additions to the Archive, but the analysis of this material unfortunately remains for happier times.

Place-name studies then are somewhat neglected, and I fear the same is true of the Older Scottish Textual Archive,[17] my computer archive of Older Scots, which remains much as it was in 1971. But happily there is booming activity elsewhere (far more than there was five years ago) in the other areas I've mentioned. Quite a number of people are devoting in a variety of ways, some of them new ways, a good deal of time, energy and knowledge to the study of Scots. A larger number of Scottish undergraduates are studying Scots to quite an advanced level in two of our universities, and in other educational institutions people are hearing about it and discussing it to an extent that did not happen before.

But of course, as who should know better than an editor of the *Dictionary of the Older Scottish Tongue,* there is a vast amount still to do. In every area of the history and present state of Scots our knowledge is still sketchy or superficial: there are original Ph D topics going galore. Yet I myself have in the last few years had several good students who wanted to do postgraduate work on Scots and were unable to raise the funds to do so. These were people who just missed being among the *crème de la crème* who get State or University or Carnegie postgraduate scholarships. What I dream of is the provision, by one of the Scottish foundations, of scholarships which are earmarked for Scottish humanistic studies.

Finally, I want to say again, as I said in 1971, however untimely this may seem in present circumstances, that we must have more teaching posts in Scots language in more universities. The subject is big enough and of sufficient importance for Scotland and for English studies in general, to deserve this of universities within and even, dare one say it, without Scotland (Ulster I would have thought, obviously). And it is also true that, as a result of some of the events I have been talking of, we are now turning out from some of our universities one or two graduates who would be worthy candidates for such posts if only they existed.

1 The Association for Scottish Literary Studies (ASLS) publishes *Scottish Literary Journal* and an annual volume (normally a work of Scottish literature which is at once important and hitherto obscure or difficult to obtain, such as *The Three Perils of Man* by James Hogg (1822), the first of these volumes), and has also published booklets of Occasional Papers, including Aitken 1973a, McClure 1974a. Its treasurer is Dr David Hewitt, Department of English, University of Aberdeen, Old Aberdeen AB9 2UB.

2 Graham Stephen, *Scotscape* (Edinburgh: Oliver and Boyd, 1978).

3 Scottish Education Department, *Scottish Literature in the Secondary School* (Edinburgh: HMSO, 1976) pp 105–111.

4 e.g. Tom Leonard, Edwin Morgan, Stephen Mulrine.

5 e.g. William McIlvanney, Alex Hamilton—see *Three Glasgow Writers* (Glasgow: Molendinar Press, 1976)—Allan Spence, Jake Flower (Alan Bold).

6 James Patrick, *A Glasgow Gang Observed* (London: Eyre Methuen, 1973).

7 e.g. *Willie Rough* and *Benny Lynch*, both by Bill Bryden, and *The Bevellers*, by Roddy McMillan (all published in Edinburgh by Southside, respectively 1972, 1975, 1974).

8 Scotsoun, 13 Ashton Road, Glasgow G12 8SP.

9 Scotsway Publications, 54 Glassel Park Road, Longniddry, East Lothian. Among these is *Introducing Scots*, a beginners' introduction to Scots for foreign residents in Scotland.

10 Adam McNaughtan, *The Glasgow that I used to know* (Caley, 1975), including McNaughtan's celebrated 'Jeely Piece Song'.

11 For a number of writings on aspects of lexicography based on one or both of the large Scottish dictionaries and for accounts of

particular dictionaries, see Aitken 1973b, c, d, e, 1975 and 1977b; Burchfield 1975; Fenton 1974; MacDiarmid 1975; Meier 1969; Murison 1972.

12 See Graham Nixon, 'Aims and Methodology of the British Urban Linguistic Survey', in Reid 1976b.

13 Subsequently printed as: Peter Trudgill, *The Social Differentiation of English in Norwich* (Cambridge University Press, 1974).

14 These include:

a sociolinguistic investigation of Edinburgh speech (David Abercrombie, Suzanne Romaine, Department of Linguistics, University of Edinburgh); supported by the Social Science Research Council;

a study of articulatory setting in the Edinburgh community (John Esling); for a Ph D in the Department of Linguistics, University of Edinburgh: see Esling 1976;

a sociolinguistic and comparative study of the speech of certain Scottish and English border towns (Paul Johnson); for a Ph D in the Department of Linguistics, University of Edinburgh;

a study of attitudes to optional lexical and grammatical usages in Edinburgh (K I Sandred, Department of English, Uppsala University);

a study of the place of Scots in Scottish education (I K Williamson); for a Ph D in the Department of English Language, University of Edinburgh.

15 Recently also Mr Richard E Wood of Adelphi University, Garden City, NY 11530, has produced a number of short articles on the current language situation in (especially Lowland) Scotland, including one on the prospects for 'language planning' in Scotland: Wood 1977a, b, c. Still more recently, a conference on Language Planning for Lowland Scots has been held in Glasgow under the auspices of ASLS and the Department of Extra-Mural and Adult Education, University of Glasgow: see p 159.

16 Further studies under way include:

a study of aspects of the syntax of Scottish English, especially of modal verbs and relative constructions (E K Brown, J Miller, M Millar, Department of Linguistics, University of Edinburgh); supported by the Social Science Research Council;

studies in the intonation of Scottish English (Gillian Brown, Karen Currie, Joanne Kenworthy, N Mitchison, Department of Linguistics, University of Edinburgh); supported by the Social Science Research Council (see also Kenworthy 1977);

studies in the orthography of pre-literary Scots and Older Scots, including /hw/ and /kw/, and other aspects of pre-literary Scots

(C D Jeffery, Department of Old and Middle English, University College, Dublin);

studies in the grammar of twentieth century literary Scots (John Kirk, Department of English, University of Bonn);

a linguistic and stylistic study of recent Scots prose (Caroline McAfee); for a Ph D in the Department of English Language, University of Edinburgh.

17 See *A Dictionary of the Older Scottish Tongue* vol IV, M–N (University of Chicago Press, 1973) p vi, for a description.

Bibliography to Chapter 8

Of published writings on Scots subsequent to Murison 1967, except *The Scottish National Dictionary* and *A Dictionary of the Older Scottish Tongue*, on which see above, pp 143–144.

Bibliographies of writings on Scots appear also in *Reader's Guide to Scotland: a Bibliography* (The National Book League 1968), 52–54, and *Lowland Scots* (Aitken 1973a), 69–71. See also the annotations in Aitken 1971, Bitterling 1970, Glauser 1974, Mather & Speitel 1975, Introduction, and Speitel & Mather 1968.

Descriptive reports on writings on Scots by J Derrick McClure have appeared regularly since 1974 in *Scottish Literary News* 3, No 4, 5–9, and in *Scottish Literary Journal*, Supplements No 1, 1975, 6–12; No 2, 1976, 1–8; No 4, 1977, 1–9. Notices of writings on language also appear in earlier 'Year's Work' reports on Scottish literature, in *Scottish Literary News* 2 and 3.

Even within its limited chronological span the present list cannot pretend to be exhaustive. For one thing there are problems of demarcation with writings mainly on other topics, especially Scottish literature, which I have arbitrarily resolved. For another, I have not attempted to include unpublished dissertations, other than those mentioned or alluded to in my text, book reviews, quite numerous articles and correspondence in newspapers and journals, minor word-books (Burns 'dictionaries' and the like), and I have arbitrarily omitted some short discursive pieces in literary and general periodicals, such as *Akros, Catalyst, The New Shetlander* and *Scotia Review*. I have not attempted to take in brief exegetical or elucidatory notes on lines or passages of Scottish literature. Extended studies on Scottish literary topics, anthologies of Scottish literature, and general histories of English or of Scotland, all almost inevitably include either sections on or allusions to the Scottish vernacular: examples of the first three of these are, respectively, Priscilla Bawcutt *Gavin Douglas* (Edinburgh University Press, 1976), John and Winifred MacQueen *A Choice of Scottish Verse 1470–1570* (Faber, 1972), and Barbara M H Strang *A History of English*

(Methuen, 1970). Except when these contain a substantial separate section on Scots language or language and style, or are mentioned in my text, I have not attempted their inclusion. Nor are reprints of earlier works included: an example is Edwin Morgan 'Dunbar and the language of poetry', originally published in 1952, reprinted in his *Essays*, 1974.

For fuller listings which include some of the omitted items, see *Annual Bibliography of Scottish Literature*, 1969–, published as an annual supplement to *The Bibliotheck*.

For a bibliography of Scottish place-name studies the reader is referred to Nicolaisen 1976, xi–xxi.

Abercrombie, D 1977. The accents of Standard English in Scotland *Work in Progress* No **10**, 21–32. Edinburgh University Linguistics Department.

Aitken, A J 1971. Variation and variety in written Middle Scots. In A J Aitken, A McIntosh & H Pálsson (eds), *Edinburgh Studies in English and Scots*, 177–209. London: Longman.

Aitken, A J 1972a. The present state of Scottish Language studies *Scottish Literary News* **March 1972**, 34–44.

Aitken, A J 1972b. Gaelic, Scots and Gullane *Scottish Literary News* **March 1972**, 45–46.

Aitken, A J (ed) 1973a. *Lowland Scots*. Edinburgh: Association for Scottish Literary Studies Occasional Papers No 2.

Aitken, A J 1973b. Sense-analysis for a historical dictionary. In H Scholler & J Reidy (eds) *Lexicography and Dialect Geography*: *Festgabe for Hans Kurath*, 5–16. Wiesbaden: Franz Steiner Verlag.

Aitken, A J 1973c. Definitions and citations in a period dictionary. In Raven I McDavid Jr & Audrey R Duckert (eds), *Lexicography in English*, 259–265. Annals of the New York Academy of Sciences, vol 211.

Aitken, A J 1973d. Le dictionnaire d'ancien écossais: aperçu de son histoire. In *Tavola Rotonda sui Grandi Lessici Storici*, 37–44. Firenze: Accademia della Crusca.

Aitken, A J 1973e. L'analyse des sens pour un dictionnaire historique. In *Tavola Rotonda sui Grandi Lessici Storici*, 91–95. Firenze: Accademia della Crusca.

Aitken, A J 1975. *The Scottish National Dictionary*. *The Scottish Review* **1**, 17–19.

Aitken, A J 1976. The Scots language and the teacher of English in Scotland. In *Scottish Literature in the Secondary School*, 48–55. Edinburgh: Scottish Education Department.

Aitken, A J 1977a. How to pronounce older Scots. In Aitken *et al* 1977, 1–21.

Aitken, A J 1977b. Textual problems and the *Dictionary of the Older*

Scottish Tongue. In P G J van Sterkenburg (ed), *Lexicologie: een bundel opstellen voor F de Tollenaere*, 13–15. Groningen: Wolters-Noordhoff.

Aitken, A J, McDiarmid, Matthew P & Thomson, Derick S (eds) 1977. *Bards and Makars: Scottish Language and Literature, Medieval and Renaissance*. Glasgow University Press.

Annand, J K 1977. The vocabulary of Hugh MacDiarmid's Scots poems *Akros* **12**, Nos 34–35, 15–19.

Bähr, Dieter 1970. Gibt es einen standardisierten Haupttonvokalismus im Schottischen Englisch? *Zeitschrift für Dialektologie und Linguistik* **37**, 337–341.

Bähr, Dieter 1974. Die Englische Sprache in Schottland, ch III of *Standard English und seine geographischen Varianten*, 127–174. München: Wilhelm Fink Verlag.

Barber, Charles 1976. The Scots literary language. In *Early Modern English*, 27–37. London: André Deutsch.

Bawcutt, Priscilla 1967. *The Palice of Honour*: Style, Verse; and *King Hart*: Form and Style, Verse, Date. In Introduction to *The Shorter Poems of Gavin Douglas*, xlv–lii; lxvi–lxxix. Edinburgh: Scottish Text Society.

Bawcutt, Priscilla 1971. Lexical notes on Gavin Douglas's *Eneados*. *Medium Ævum* **40**, 48–55.

Bernhart, Walter 1978. The rising incubus: a view from Alpine regions *Akros* **13**, No 38, 113–119.

Bitterling, K 1970. *Der Wortschatz von Barbours 'Bruce'*. Ph D dissertation, Free University of Berlin.

Bitterling, K 1975. Till 'while' in Barbours *Bruce*. *Neuphilologische Mitteilungen* **76**, 428.

Borrowman, Lorna 1977. The Scots tongue in education *Akros* **11**, No 33, 107–118.

Boutelle, Ann E 1971. Language and vision in the early poetry of Hugh MacDiarmid *Contemporary Literature* **12**, 495–509.

Bozek, Philip 1976. Hugh MacDiarmid's early lyrics: a syntactic examination *Language and Style* **9**, 29–41.

Brown, E K & Millar, Martin 1978. Auxiliary Verbs in Edinburgh Speech *Work in Progress* No 11, 146–184. Edinburgh University Linguistics Department.

Brown, E K & Miller, J 1975. Modal verbs in Scottish English *Work in Progress* No **8**, 99–114. Edinburgh University Linguistics Department.

Burchfield, R W 1975. Ayr., Ork., and a' that *The Scottish Review* **1**, 20–21.

Buthlay, Kenneth 1977. Shibboleths of the Scots in the poetry of Hugh MacDiarmid *Akros* **12**, Nos 34–35, 23–47.

Cairns, Robert 1974. The languages of Scotland *Scotia Review* **6**, 20–26.

Caldwell, Sarah J G 1967. *The Relative Pronoun in Early Scots: a*

Lexicographical and Syntactical Study. Ph D thesis, University of Edinburgh.

Caldwell, Sarah J G 1974. *The Relative Pronoun in Early Scots* Mémoires de la Société Néophilologique de Helsinki, 42.

Campbell, Donald 1975. Modren Scots *Lallans* 5, 29–30.

Cheyne, W M 1971. Stereotyped reactions to speakers with Scottish and English regional accents *British Journal of Social and Clinical Psychology* 9, 77–79.

Conley, John 1968. William Dunbar: additions to and corrections of *O E D* and *D O S T*. *Notes and Queries* May 1968, 169–172.

Dorian, Nancy C 1970a. East Sutherland by-naming *Scottish Studies* 14, 59–65.

Dorian, Nancy C 1970b. A substitute name-system in the Scottish Highlands *American Anthropologist* 72, 303–319.

Ellenberger, B 1977. *The Latin Element in the Vocabulary of the Earlier Makars, Henryson and Dunbar*. Lund Studies in English 51. Gleerup: C W K.

Esling, John 1976. Articulatory setting in the community. In Reid 1976b, 19–20.

Ewen, C J 1977. Aitken's Law and the phonatory gesture in dependency phonology *Lingua* 41, 307–329.

Fenton, A 1970a. The plough-song: a Scottish source for medieval plough history *Tools and Tillage* 1, 175–191.

Fenton, A 1970b. The tabu language of Shetland Fishermen *Ethnologia Europaea* 2–3, 118–122.

Fenton, A 1973. *The Various Names of Shetland* Edinburgh: Blackwood.

Fenton, A 1974. Lexicography and historical interpretation. In G W S Barrow (ed) *The Scottish Tradition: Essays in Honour of R G Cant*, 243–258. Edinburgh: Scottish Academic Press.

Fenton, A 1978. *The Northern Isles: Orkney and Shetland*. Scots lexicographic material *passim* and, in particular, Terminology of the one-stilted plough (304–306), List of sheep-marks 1934 (473–474), Terminology of sheep marks (484–490) and The sea-language of fishermen and the end of Norn (ch 70, 616–622). John Donald.

Fraser, Kenneth C 1974. The rebirth o Scots *Scotia Review* 6, 32–35.

Glauser, B 1974. *The Scottish-English Linguistic Border: Lexical Aspects*. The Cooper Monographs. Bern: Francke Verlag.

Glen, Duncan 1970. The spelling of Scots *Scotia* 3, 1–4.

Gordon, C D 1970. Gavin Douglas's Latin vocabulary *Phoenix* 24, 54–73.

Gore, Charles 1969. Remnants of Scottish life and character. In Alan S C Ross (ed), *What are U?*, 97–115, esp. 109–113. London: André Deutsch.

Graham, William 1974–1976. Teach yourself Lallans *Lallans* 3, 17–19; 4, 23–25; 5, 26–28; 6, 25–27.

Graham, William 1976–1978. Teach yourself Scots *Lallans* **7**, 27–29; **8**, 28–30; **9**, 25–27.

Graham, William 1977. *The Scots Word Book* Edinburgh: Ramsay Head Press.

Gussenhoven, C & Broeders, A 1976. Scots English. In *The Pronunciation of English*, 201–209. Groningen: Wolters-Noordhoff/Longman.

Hanham, Alison 1969. 'The Scottish Hecate': a wild witch chase *Scottish Studies* **13**, 59–65.

'Henryson, Robert' 1978. A Scottish Viewpoint II: a new sang for an auld leid. An interview with Mr Robert Henryson, Principal Teacher of English, Spens Academy, Fife, conducted by an Uphauder (Official) of the Society of Lowland Scottish Studies *Akros* **13**, No 37, 40–51.

Herdman, John 1972. The progress of Scots *Akros* **7**, No 20, 31–42.

Jamieson, Peter 1974. Sea-speech and beliefs of Shetland fishermen (Part 1) *The New Shetlander* **110**, 30–32.

Kenworthy, Joanne 1977. The intonation of questions in one variety of Scottish English *Work in Progress* No **10**, 70–81. Edinburgh University Linguistics Department.

Kohler, K J 1968. Aspects of Middle Scots phonemics and graphemics: the phonological implications of the sign ⟨i⟩ *Transactions of the Philological Society* **1967**, 32–61.

Lass, Roger 1973. A case for making phonological rules state things that don't happen *Edinburgh Working Papers in Linguistics* **3**, 10–18. Edinburgh University English Language & Linguistics Departments.

Lass, Roger 1974. Linguistic orthogenesis? Scots vowel quantity and the English length conspiracy. In J M Anderson & C Jones (eds), *Historical Linguistics*, vol 2, 311–343. Amsterdam: North-Holland Publishing Company.

Lass, Roger 1976. *English Phonology and Phonological Theory: Synchronic and Diachronic Studies.* Cambridge University Press.

Leisi, E 1969. *Das heutige Englisch: Wesenszüge und Probleme*, 180. 5 Aufl., Heidelberg.

Low, John T 1974. Scots in education: the contemporary situation. In McClure 1974a, 17–27.

Macaulay, R K S 1973. Double standards *American Anthropology* **75**, 1324–1337.

Macaulay, R K S 1974. Linguistic insecurity. In McClure 1974a, 35–43.

Macaulay, R K S 1975. Negative prestige, linguistic insecurity and linguistic self-hatred *Lingua* **36**, 147–161.

Macaulay, R K S 1976. Social class and language in Glasgow *Language in Society* **5**, 173–188.

Macaulay, R K S 1977. *Language, Social Class and Education: a*

Glasgow Study [Revised version of Macaulay & Trevelyan 1973].
Edinburgh University Press.

Macaulay, R K S 1978. Variation and consistency in Glaswegian
English. In Trudgill 1978, 132–143.

Macaulay, R K S & Trevelyan, Gavin D 1973. *Language, Education
and Employment in Glasgow*: report to the Social Science
Research Council. Edinburgh: Scottish Council for Research in
Education.

McClure, J Derrick 1970. *Some Features of Standard English as
spoken in Southwest Scotland*. M Litt thesis, University of Edinburgh.

McClure, J Derrick 1971–1972. Dialect in *The House with the Green
Shutters. Studies in Scottish Literature* 9, 148–163.

McClure, J Derrick (ed) 1974a. *The Scots Language in Education*.
Aberdeen: Association for Scottish Literary Studies Occasional
Papers No 3.

McClure, J Derrick 1974b. Modern Scots prose-writing. In McClure
1974a, 54–67.

McClure, J Derrick 1974c. Suas Leis an Albannaich *Lallans* 3,
20–22.

McClure, J Derrick 1975. The English Speech of Scotland *The
Aberdeen University Review* 46, 173–189.

McClure, J Derrick 1976. Fae A til Zulu *Lallans* 7, 24–26.

McClure, J Derrick 1977. Vowel duration in a Scottish accent
Journal of the International Phonetic Association 7, 10–16.

MacDiarmid, Hugh 1975. The foundation stone of the new Scotland
[on David Murison and *The Scottish National Dictionary*]. *The
Scottish Review* 1, 21–25.

McDiarmid, Matthew P 1973. Language. In *The Kingis Quair of
James Stewart*, 7–28. London: Heinemann.

McIntosh, Angus 1978. The dialectology of Medieval Scots: some
possible approaches to its study. In Speitel 1978a, 38–44.

Mackay, Margaret A 1973. The Scots of the Makars. In Aitken
1973a, 20–37.

Mackay, Margaret A 1975. *The Alliterative Tradition in Middle Scots*.
Ph D thesis, University of Edinburgh.

McNeill, Peter & Nicholson, Ranald 1975. *An Historical Atlas of
Scotland c400–c1600*. St Andrews: Atlas Committee of the
Conference of Scottish Medievalists.

Mather, James Y 1966. Aspects of the linguistic geography of
Scotland II: East Coast fishing *Scottish Studies* 10, 129–153.

Mather, James Y 1969. Aspects of the linguistic geography of
Scotland III: Fishing communities of the East Coast (Part 1)
Scottish Studies 13, 1–16.

Mather, James Y 1972. Linguistic geography and the traditional
drift-net fishery of the Scottish East Coast. In M F Wakelin (ed)
Patterns in the Folk Speech of the British Isles, 7–31. London:

Athlone Press.

Mather, James Y 1973. The Scots we speak today. In Aitken 1973a, 56–68.

Mather, James Y 1974. Social variation in present-day Scots speech. In McClure 1974a, 44–53.

Mather, James Y 1978. The dialect of Caithness. In Speitel 1978a, 1–16.

Mather, James Y & Speitel, H H (eds) 1975/1977. *The Linguistic Atlas of Scotland*, Scots Section vols 1 & 2. London: Croom Helm.

Meier, H H 1969. Lexicography as applied linguistics *English Studies* **50**, 141–151.

Meier, H H 1977. Scots is not alone: the Swiss and Low German analogues. In Aitken *et al* 1977, 201–213.

Mulder, Jan W F 1974. Descriptive adequacy in phonology and the vowel phonemes of the Scottish dialects of Angus and Perthshire compared with the Southern English system *La Linguistique* **10**, 71–91.

Murison, David 1967. A survey of Scottish Language studies *Forum for Modern Language Studies* **3**, 276–285.

Murison, David 1970. The two languages of Scott. In A N Jeffares (ed), *Scott's Mind and Art*, 206–229. Edinburgh: Oliver & Boyd.

Murison, David 1971a. The future of Scots. In Duncan Glen (ed), *Whither Scotland*, 159–177. London: Gollancz.

Murison, David 1971b. The Dutch element in the vocabulary of Scots. In A J Aitken, A McIntosh & H Pálsson (eds), *Edinburgh Studies in English and Scots*, 159–176. London:Longman.

Murison, David 1972. *The Scottish National Dictionary. University of Edinburgh Journal* **25**, 305–309.

Murison, David 1974a. Linguistic relationships in medieval Scotland. In G W S Barrow (ed), *The Scottish Tradition: Essays in Honour of R G Cant*, 71–83. Edinburgh: Scottish Academic Press.

Murison, David 1974b. The vocabulary of the Kirk (Part 1) *Liturgical Review* **4**, 2: 45–49.

Murison, David 1975a. The vocabulary of the Kirk (Part 2) *Liturgical Review* **5**, 1: 53–55.

Murison, David 1975b. The language of Sydney Goodsir Smith. In *For Sydney Goodsir Smith*, 23–29. Edinburgh: M Macdonald.

Murison, David 1976a. The language of Burns. In Donald A Low (ed), *Critical Essays on Robert Burns*, 54–69. London: Routledge & Kegan Paul.

Murison, David 1976b. The speech of Moray. In Donald Omand (ed), *The Moray Book*, 275–282. Edinburgh: Paul Harris.

Murison, David 1977. *The Guid Scots Tongue*. Edinburgh: Blackwood.

Murison, David, 1978. The language of the ballads. In Speitel 1978a, 54–64.

Mutt, Oleg 1977. Scottish English. In *Social and Regional Varieties of Present-day English*. Tartu State University, Department of English Studies.

Neill, William 1970. Language and Scotland *Catalyst* 3, Spring, 10–11.

Neill, William 1976. Heat, light and language *Scotia Review* 12, 33–36.

Nicolaisen, W F H 1976. *Scottish Place-Names*. London: Batsford.

Nicolaisen, W F H 1977. Line and sentence in Dunbar's poetry. In Aitken *et al* 1977, 61–71.

Pride, Glen L 1975. *Glossary of Scottish Building*. Glasgow: Scottish Civic Trust.

Purves, David 1974. Economical Scots *Lallans* 3, 22–23.

Purves, David 1975. The spelling of Scots *Lallans* 4, 26–27.

Reid, Euan 1975. Social and stylistic variation in the speech of some eleven-year-old Edinburgh boys *Work in Progress* No 8, 124–126. Edinburgh University Linguistics Department.

Reid, Euan 1976a *Social and Stylistic Variation in the Speech of Some Edinburgh Schoolchildren*. M Litt thesis, University of Edinburgh.

Reid, Euan (ed) 1976b. *Abstracts of 1976 Research Seminar on Sociolinguistic Variation*. Walsall: West Midlands College, Communications Research Unit.

Reid, Euan 1976c. Social and stylistic variation in the speech of some Edinburgh schoolchildren. In Reid 1976b, 16.

Reid, Euan 1978. Social and stylistic variation in the speech of children: some evidence from Edinburgh. In Trudgill 1978, 158–171.

Robertson, T 1970. Extracts from a Shetland Dictionary under preparation *The New Shetlander* 92, 35–36; 93, 28.

Robertson, T 1974. Shetland dialect *The New Shetlander* 107, 8–10.

Robinson, Mairi 1973. Modern literary Scots: Fergusson and after. In Aitken 1973a, 38–55.

Romaine, Suzanne 1975a. *Linguistic Variability in the Speech of Some Edinburgh Schoolchildren*. M Litt thesis, University of Edinburgh.

Romaine, Suzanne 1975b. Approaches to the description of Scots English *Work in Progress* No 8, 121–124. Edinburgh University Linguistics Department.

Romaine, Suzanne 1978. Postvocalic /r/ in Scottish English: sound change in progress? In Trudgill 1978, 144–157.

Romaine, Suzanne & Reid, Euan 1976. Glottal sloppiness? A sociolinguistic view of urban speech in Scotland *Teaching English* 9, 12–17. Edinburgh; Moray House College of Education: Centre for Information on the Teaching of English.

Ross, Alan S C 1968. 'You' in the North *Notes and Queries* **September 1968**, 323–324.

Ross, J 1972. A selection of Caithness dialect words. In Donald

Omand (ed), *The Caithness Book*, 241–260. Inverness: Highland Printers Ltd.

Samuels, M L 1972. *Linguistic Evolution, with Special Reference to English*. Cambridge University Press.

Scur, G S 1968. On the non-finite forms of the verb *can* in Scottish *Acta Linguistica Hafniensia* **11**, 211–218.

Simon, J R 1967. Etude graphématique, Etude morphologique, Etude syntaxique, Le style, La versification. In *Le Livre du Roi*, 35–202. Paris: Aubier–Montaigne.

Speitel, H H 1969a. *Some Studies in the Dialect of Midlothian*. Ph D thesis, University of Edinburgh.

Speitel, H H 1969b. An areal typology of isoglosses: isoglosses near the Scottish-English border *Zeitschrift für Mundartforschung* **36**, 49–66.

Speitel, H H 1969c. An early specimen of Edinburgh speech *Work in Progress* No **3**, 26–36. Edinburgh University Linguistics Department.

Speitel, H H 1972. The stressed vowels in Standard Scottish English: a reply to D Baehr *Zeitschrift für Dialektologie und Linguistik* **39**, 215–216.

Speitel, H H 1975a. Dialect. In A Davies (ed), *Problems of Language and Learning*, 34–60. London: Heinemann.

Speitel, H H 1975b. 'Caller Ou!' An Edinburgh fishwives' cry and an old Scottish sound change *Scottish Studies* **19**, 69–73.

Speitel, H H (ed) 1978a. *Scottish Literary Journal* Supplement No 6, Spring 1978.

Speitel, H H 1978b. The word geography of the Borders. In Speitel 1978a, 17–37.

Speitel, H H & Mather, James Y 1968. Schottische Dialektologie. In *Germanische Dialektologie: Festschrift für Walter Mitzka zum 80 Geburtstag*, 520–541. *Zeitschrift für Mundartforschung*, Neue Folge 6.

(Taylor) Mary Vaiana 1972. *A Study in the Dialect of the Southern Counties of Scotland*. Ph D thesis, Indiana University.

Taylor, Mary Vaiana 1974. The great Southern Scots conspiracy: patterns in the development of Northern English. In J M Anderson & C Jones (eds), *Historical Linguistics* vol 2, 403–426. Amsterdam: North-Holland Publishing Company.

Templeton, Janet M 1973. Scots: an outline history. In Aitken 1973a, 4–19.

Trengove, Graham 1975. Who is you? Grammar and Grassic Gibbon *Scottish Literary Journal* **2**, 47–62.

Trudgill, Peter 1974. Sociolinguistics and Scots dialects. In McClure 1974a, 28–34.

Trudgill, Peter 1978. *Sociolinguistic Patterns in British English*. London: Edward Arnold.

Wells, J C 1971. A Scots diphthong and the feature 'continuant' *Journal* of the International Phonetic Association **1**, 29–32.

Welsh, Alexander 1973. Contrast of styles in the Waverley Novels *Novel* **6**, 218–228.

Williamson, May G 1978. Place names of the Scottish Borders. In Speitel 1978a, 44–53.

Winston, Millicent 1971. *Some Aspects of the Pronunciation of Educated Scots*. M Litt thesis, University of Edinburgh.

Withrington, Donald J 1974. Scots in education: a historical retrospect. In McClure 1974a, 9–16.

Wood, Richard E 1977a. Potential issues for language planning in Scotland *Language Planning Newsletter* **3**, No 1. Honolulu: East-West Culture Learning Institute.

Wood, Richard E 1977b. Sociolinguistics in Scotland *Sociolinguistic Newsletter* **VIII**, 3–9.

Wood, Richard E 1977c. Linguistic organisations in Scotland *Language Problems and Language Planning* **1**.

Recent Conferences on Scots Language

20 November 1971, in the University of Edinburgh: *Scottish Language* (Association for Scottish Literary Studies). *Publication—* Aitken 1972a.

12–13 May 1972, in the University of Edinburgh: *Lowland Scots* (Department of Educational Studies, University of Edinburgh; Moray House College of Education; and Association for Scottish Literary Studies). *Publication—*Aitken 1973a (and see Templeton 1973, Mackay 1973, Robinson 1973 and Mather 1973).

6–9 April 1973, in the University of Edinburgh: *The Linguistic Study of Lowland Scots* (Department of Educational Studies, University of Edinburgh; and Association for Scottish Literary Studies). *Publication—*McClure 1975.

27 April 1974, in Old Gala House, Galashiels: *Lowland Scots* (Department of Educational Studies, University of Edinburgh; Association for Scottish Literary Studies; and Selkirk County Council Education Committee).

28 June–1 July 1974, in Aberdeen College of Education: *The Scots Language in Education* (Aberdeen College of Education and Association for Scottish Literary Studies). *Publication—*McClure 1974a (and see Withrington 1974, Low 1974, Trudgill 1974, Macaulay 1974, Mather 1974 and McClure 1974b).

26 April 1975, in the Community Centre, Berwick upon Tweed: *The Language of the Eastern Borders* (Department of Adult Education,

University of Newcastle upon Tyne; and Association for Scottish Literary Studies).

15 November 1975, in the University of Glasgow: *English As We Speak It In Scotland* (Department of Extra-mural and Adult Education, University of Glasgow; and Association for Scottish Literary Studies). *Publication*—the present volume.

5–6 June 1976, in the University of Stirling: *The Scots Tongue in Education* (Lallans Society—now Scots Language Society—Fifth Annual Conference). *Publication*—Borrowman 1977.

5–9 July 1976, in Hamilton College of Education: *The Language of Children in Scottish Primary Schools* (Hamilton College of Education and Association for Scottish Literary Studies).

13 November 1976, in the University of Glasgow: *Scotland's Languages: the Contemporary Situation* (Department of Extra-mural and Adult Education, University of Glasgow). *Publication*—the present volume.

23 April 1977, in the Technical College, Thurso: *The Language and Literature of Northern Scotland* (Department of Adult Education and Extra-mural Studies, University of Aberdeen; and Association for Scottish Literary Studies). *Publication*—Mather 1978.

15 October 1977, in the Scottish College of Textiles, Galashiels: *The Language of the Borders* (Department of Extra-Mural Studies, University of Edinburgh; and Association for Scottish Literary Studies). *Publication*—Murison 1978, Speitel 1978b, Williamson 1978 (all in Speitel 1978a).

19 November 1977, in the University of Glasgow: *Language Planning for Lowland Scots* (Department of Extra-mural and Adult Education, University of Glasgow; and Association for Scottish Literary Studies).

6th May 1978, in the Cabarfeidh Hotel, Golspie: *Language and Folklore in Sutherland* (Department of Adult Education and Extra-Mural Studies, University of Aberdeen; and Association for Scottish Literary Studies).

6th May 1978, in Craiglockhart College of Education: *The Scots Language in Schools* (Committee for the Advancement of Scottish Literature in Schools; and Craiglockhart College of Education).

30 September 1978, in the University of Edinburgh: *Language Variety in the Edinburgh Area* (Department of Extra-Mural Studies, University of Edinburgh; and Association for Scottish Literary Studies).

30 September 1978, in the Royal Hotel, Kirkwall: *The Dialect, Place-names and Folklore of Orkney* (Department of Adult Educa-

tion and Extra-Mural Studies, University of Aberdeen; and Association for Scottish Literary Studies).

18 November 1978, in the University of Glasgow: *The Place of the Scots Language in the S C E Examinations* (Department of Adult and Continuing Education, University of Glasgow; and Association for Scottish Literary Studies).